CONT

BODY AND MIND READING

READING

 a beginner's guide

KRISTYNA ARCARTI

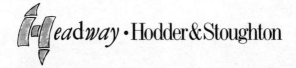

Order queries: please contact Bookpoint Ltd, 39 Milton Park, Abingdon, Oxon
OX14 4TD. Telephone: (44) 01235 400414, Fax: (44) 01235 400454. Lines are open
from 9.00 - 6.00, Monday to Saturday, with a 24 hour message answering service.
Email address: orders@bookpoint.co.uk

British Library Cataloguing in Publication Data
A catalogue record for this title is available from The British Library

ISBN 0 340 73063 3

First published 1999
Impression number 10 9 8 7 6 5 4 3 2 1
Year   2004 2003 2002 2001 2000 1999

Typeset by Transet Limited, Coventry, England.
Printed in Great Britain for Hodder & Stoughton Educational, a division of Hodder
Headline plc, 338 Euston Road, London NW1 3BH by Cox and Wyman Limited,
Reading, Berks.

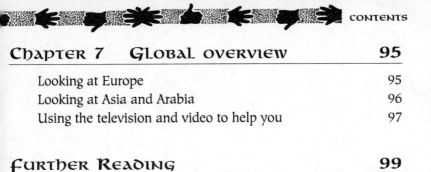

INTRODUCTION

'No man is an island' the saying goes, and it is true that even in the case of people who prefer their own company, we all meet people in our daily lives and form relationships of one sort of another with them.

There are, of course, a huge variety of relationships. There are work relationships, those people we meet daily at work but with whom we don't tend to socialise outside of the workplace. Then there are various types of social and personal relationships and also, of course, more intimate relationships. Most relationships start out being based on what we say to each other, but sometimes, words mislead us and we can receive clearer information from body language.

This book is aimed at those people who are interested in learning what the unspoken physical messages are, especially where relationships are concerned. As with all books within this series, this is merely an introduction to the subject of body language, and those people who then find the subject worthy of further investigation will find a further reading section at the back of the book.

WHAT IS BODY LANGUAGE?

If you look in the dictionary to see what the definition of body language is, you will read that body language is all about how we transmit signals to one another without verbal communication. In other words it is non-verbal communication. Verbal communication is all about speaking and listening, reading and writing. Non-verbal communication is all about posture, facial expression and gestures, and does not make use of language, in either its written or spoken form. However, as far as studying body language goes, it is important to include both verbal communication and non-verbal in order to formulate a fully rounded judgement. We must also take into account the situation and our knowledge of the person or persons with whom we are interacting, as well as look at the combination of all the signals, from face, hands, body posture and what is said to avoid any incorrect conclusions being reached.

People who are deaf or hard of hearing often train themselves to be able to pick up on other signs transmitted from person to person. Many of them will learn a sign language, where hand movements and finger shapes are formed which transmit the words intended. Most of these sign languages concentrate on giving an overall picture, rather than on giving a word-by-word translation. The rest of us can watch with fascination at the skills involved, and wonder at how the picture is being conveyed. It is, however, worthwhile remembering that the language used by the deaf and hard of hearing is not non-verbal communication, because it signals letters, words and sentences, and is thus a form of verbal communication, as is the written word. Non-verbal communication can, however, replace language where there is too much noise for spoken communication

to take place, or there is a distance involved over which the sound could not possibly travel. For this reason, signals like putting a finger over the lips can be recognised as 'be quiet', and a beckoning finger as meaning 'come over here'. In a similar way, cyclists use hand signals indicating changes of direction and so on.

We all, however, pick up on sign language in other ways – the sign language of the body. Other animals have no language, but are able to communicate by using smell, touch, sight and hearing, as are we. We may prefer to use speech, but we have an ability for non-verbal communication, and often use it without it being a conscious thought process.

In body language, we will give signals of our innermost thoughts and feelings. Not only the hands will be used, but also the eyes, our stance, the way we sit, the way we smile, frown and much more besides. Even the way we walk can give clues as to our state of mind and general demeanor.

When we are sad, depressed or weighed down with problems, we naturally tend to walk along in a way different from when we are happy or joyful. Taking a look at people in the street will help you to identify different groups of people – those people who are happy will seem to have a spring in their step, probably have their heads held high, may be smiling, laughing or joking with fellow walkers. Those people who are in a hurry will be walking at a faster speed. Business men and women, often identified by their clothing, will possibly also be glancing at their watches, or be using a mobile phone and be irritated when others get in their way. Time is precious and they have to be somewhere else. Those people, however, who are unhappy will seem to walk along in a dejected way, with head probably bowed, looking at the pavement, maybe their hands will be be in their pockets, their stance will indicate the fact that they feel burdened, they look as though they have a heavy weight on their shoulders and are stooping to carry the load. They won't be smiling, they will look unhappy, their eyes (more of which later) may well indicate a sad demeanor. By the same token, someone preoccupied with a problem may also be walking with head down, but although walking slowly they will be less hunched over, more relaxed in the

arms and legs, and might even go as far as to kick at empty drinks cans or other such pieces of rubbish they come across in the street. All this we assimilate quite naturally, so in essence, we are already aware of body language and know 'signs'.

On a daily basis, we all send out messages to other people, both verbally and non-verbally and act upon how they are received – this is known as feedback. When we talk to one another, we are always looking for feedback – ask a comedian whether he knows if his performance went well or not, and he will talk about the feedback he received from the audience, which may have ranged from

laughter and applause to silence and/or people getting up and leaving or just moving around a lot in their seats. It is all about observation. Similarly, in our conversations with others, we can tell by smiles, frowns, body posture, gestures and so on whether the conversation is going well, or not, and how to progress in the interaction using this knowledge.

Most people will know the hidden signs which indicate that a person around them is in a bad mood – they will observe and act accordingly. Often another person's way of acting, even without the benefit of verbal communication, will signal that all is not well. Sometimes, a person in a bad mood will slam around, bang things down, slam doors, throw things or show some such aggressive behaviour to give a warning bell to others, whilst other people will tense up bodily, their stance will change and they will go off on their own to 'cool down'. All these things are body language signals. We just have to learn what they are, identify them and act accordingly.

Let's take a little time now to think about what we already know about other people. If you have the time, sit for a while and look at the people you already know around you. What can you tell from their behaviour at the moment. Start to think about their body language. Use them as your guinea-pigs!

Where does body language start? What can we hope to learn?

Body language starts the moment we are born, and babies will instinctively know how, for example, to indicate they are hungry, or uncomfortable. Studies have shown that children who are born both blind and deaf show basically the same facial expressions of crying, smiling and laughing as children without these handicaps, and it is

therefore obvious that we all have a knowledge of body language from the moment of birth onwards.

Parents know their baby's body language. After all, babies can't communicate their difficulties, other than by crying, but parents learn to know their baby, know whether they are uncomfortable, in distress, ill or happy by the signs their baby gives. Those of us without a detailed knowledge of babies and their behaviour can often be quite astounded how parents can pick up on the fact that little Johnny or little Sally isn't very well and a bit off colour from their body language. We might call it perception or intuition, but it is really all about learning the non-verbal clues – we all know, for example, that the eyebrows will raise when we are surprised and that the brow will furrow when we are anxious, and this book will study some more subtle ways that actions reveal hidden meanings.

We all learn as we grow, and you can watch children imitate their elders, including language which they shouldn't copy! As adults, we also pick up on other people's behaviour, and often can be influenced by those we hold in esteem or who we feel attracted to in some form. We also learn how to 'mirror image', more of which later, and it is fair to say that although some facial expressions may be with us from birth, most non-verbal communication is learnt, and some people learn more than others.

It is estimated that in excess of 90 per cent of face-to-face communication is non-verbal, and increasing studies in countries around the globe continue to give us more and more information. Studies have been continuing for more than 40 years now, and it is estimated that how we act and behave is more than 13 times as informative as what we actually say, and in excess of 1 million non-verbal signals have been recorded. Often, by just learning a little more about our body language, we can find out what attracts us to others; what image we ourselves project to others; how to react to a certain person in any given situation. As a result, we can all be more successful in our relationships, both personal, professional and occasional. However, we must remember that for successful social interaction, we need feedback in both verbal and non-verbal forms, and should realise that non-verbal communication can be correctly understood only in the total context of the situation presented at the

time, and with existing knowledge, if appropriate, of the people concerned. During the course of this book, you will see that all of us reveal a lot about ourselves by our gestures, our movements and our stance, as well as by our eyes, which are said to be the windows to the soul. More about eyes in Chapter 3.

But beware, to paraphrase Abraham Lincoln, you can fool some of the people some of the time, but you can't fool all of the people all of the time. Even those people who have studied body language and are skilled in its practice will find times when they are taken unawares by somebody, having either misread the body language signals or having failed to take into account extenuating factors. Some time ago, I remember talking to a friend who had been studying body language as part of his job. Full of enthusiasm for his newly acquired skills, he set about talking to a group of people, telling them what their body language told him. Most times he was right in his explanations. However, with one lady he was wildly inaccurate. He spent some considerable time telling her why she was sitting in a certain way and what it meant, to be told, 'Actually you are totally wrong. I'm sitting like this because I have a bad back and sitting any other way would cause me pain'.

Body language can tell us a lot, but we do need to be aware that it won't be foolproof taken in isolation. We have to also take into account what is said, what we know about the person concerned and what their personality may be. Body language knowledge will give us information slightly different from what we might pick up from merely listening to a conversation. We can learn about gestures, learn how to judge people by their behaviour and so on, and thus become a better judge of character and of people. We can pick up signs of someone who is telling lies or not telling the whole truth, and we can also learn to identify the signs of nervousness, but we will not be able to mind read, neither will we always be 100 per cent accurate. Learning about body language will not give us access to some magical formula which will revolutionise our lives and give us untold wealth and happiness. It won't ensure we have a happy relationship, it won't ensure our promotion at work, it won't ensure that the bank manager will give us the loan we have asked for.

It will, however, give us more information on how we, as a species, communicate with each other, and help us to understand ourselves and others. We won't, as a result of reading this book, be able to use body language as a manipulative tool for our own ends. Most of us can spot a fake smile. This could indicate many things from someone being unhappy at heart but putting on a show for the sake of it, to someone who is trying to mislead us, or someone who is trying to make out they are our friends when they are not, to someone who is exceptionally nervous. You have to consider other factors before making an assessment. Most of us will also know of those people who avoid eye contact, which could suggest that they might be devious, nervous, shifty or lacking in confidence. It could also, however, indicate boredom, or unhappiness, and making a firm judgement on somebody's disposition from such things in isolation can cause problems. However, all these things register, and even the most accomplished students of body language will agree that we never know it all, and can sometimes be mistaken. This leads us neatly into the next section.

Is it possible to fake body language?

How many times have you been in a situation, either personally or as a bystander, and wondered whether the person speaking is being totally honest. By the same token, how many times have we 'put on a face' in an attempt to hide our true feelings. At some time or another we all feel the need to hide our true feelings, but if you learn body language signals, you will find that we are not really as successful as we would have ourselves believe. Sometimes, after an argument with a close friend or partner our actions can seem quite placid, but our voices will have within them tell-tale signs, which, if written down, could be missed. Our intonation may not be quite right, and you can bet that, discounting the voice altogether, there will be something in our body language which will give a clue to our real feelings on the matter.

Many people are accomplished performers at speaking what is not really the truth, especially those who seek to gain some advantage over others, either singularly or *en masse* for personal gain. Often they have had years of practice and can seemingly put forward a case which is both plausible and realistic, but in fact has no basis in fact at all. Salespeople can often put forward a very good case for a product, and training courses in sales techniques will all, to some degree, focus on how to make the audience believe your sales pitch. Likewise, politicians are often adept at making the best possible case for their party. Most of them will adapt what they say and how they say it to suit their audience, altering the type of words they use, the type of gestures, as well as their clothing. They will also be well aware that their stance is important. They need to project an image that people feel they can trust. However, people often sense insincerity, we all have freedom of choice to believe what is said and what is offered, both verbally and non-verbally, and decide for ourselves. We can all be attracted to different things and repelled or put off by others. People who have a lot of charm can also be said to be 'charismatic', but it is worthwhile remembering that charm can also be the meaning for a magic spell! Likewise, where does charm end and smarm begin? Even in biblical times, the writer of Proverbs suggested that charm may be false (Proverbs 31:30), and we will take a look at deceit in a later chapter.

Generally speaking, liars talk and seem to react slowly, as if they feel it necessary to think really hard before speaking, and anything approaching normal speed of speech will trip them up. They will also speak less and can seem nervous in their actions – fiddle with things, move things about, avoid eye contact and especially body contact.

You may argue that actors can fake body language, and do so successfully all the time and, as such, so can the person in the street learn to fake body language. In the world of acting, skills are learnt which will help the audience to believe that the actor really *is* the person she is playing, but you must remember that the actor is playing a part, and even she goes home at the end of the day to a normal lifestyle, where she will behave and act as she is, naturally. You only have to think back to the silent films of earlier this century to see how good skilled actors really are with non-verbal

communication. Some actors seemed to be wooden, behaving unnaturally, or conversely behaving in extremely over-exaggerated styles. Some actors seemed more effective and plausible, but they were judged on their performance without words. As film techniques developed and sound was introduced, we probably took less notice of the non-verbal communication, preferring to listen to the dialogue, but we still tend to judge actors on their overall performance, which includes their body language, when thinking in terms of what makes a good actor. Perhaps, however, it would be a worthwhile exercise to turn off the sound when watching a film on television especially if it happens to be a film we have seen before, and just observe the action through the body language. Often, I would suggest, you will see really exaggerated actions which aren't natural, but which you would have failed to notice had the sound been turned up. This is done so that the audience will notice more, and is something that politicians and also those involved in public speaking also do, so again watch them a little more closely and see what you can pick up, because exaggerated actions, especially postural, will be quite easy to notice. It is, in fact, a very interesting and worthwhile exercise to watch politicians in television debates. On the assumption that you are not too bothered about what is being said and are prepared to concentrate your attention on the body language being shown, you will invariably see politicians tend to lean forward when speaking, both when standing and sitting, but more especially when sitting. Any handshake given will appear to be firm and confident, they will nod their heads quite a lot when listening, to show they they are interested in the other person's view or question, and they will endeavour to smile as much as possible. Eye contact will be more than normal and they will prefer to have the lower part of their body obscured by a table or a rostrum as, generally speaking, more will be 'given away' by their lower body language than their upper body language. Shuffling, altering stance, moving feet or, if sitting, crossing and uncrossing the legs can all be give-aways about our true feelings, as we will see as we progress.

Most of us will admit to having 'gut feelings' about things, including people. We have this inner ability to be able to spot the fake, the falsehood, the liar. It is suggested by many that women are more able to do this, possibly because of their more emotional makeup,

and as such the term 'woman's intuition' has been coined. Men, however, are also quite adept at picking up on situations, and both genders have what seem to be inbuilt abilities to know what is happening from considering body language, possibly learnt from observation of others from an early age. So then, even if we give out signals of honesty and openness, something will give us away. Our gestures may be indicative of honesty, but there will be something which won't match up, even if this takes a while to show through. Even the most accomplished liars can be spotted by those with a thorough knowledge of body language. People who lie often try to disguise their natural body language. They turn away slightly, or stand unusually still, as if they have rehearsed their speech beforehand in front of a mirror with limited view. Most liars try to fix their facial expressions to neutral, but try to maintain eye contact and smile a lot to fool us. However, the smile won't seem natural and the eyes will remain unsmiling. Those who lie infrequently, who have a conscience which pricks or who feel generally uncomfortable with the lie may clench their hands or move their fingers around a lot. They may also be nervous with their foot movements and their breathing may seem unnatural. When we are nervous, many of us experience the 'dry mouth' syndrome. Those of us who have spoken in front of large audiences will be well aware of this, and seek to have a glass of water readily available. By the same token, people who feel nervous about lying may also seek to have liquid refreshment available. However, well-practised liars will be aware of this, and seek to stand perfectly still and show no such 'give-away' signals. Most liars though, over a period of time, especially if challenged, will emit true body signals, especially if looked at impassively straight in the eyes. Maybe such people should consider writing letters to convey their message or stick to using the telephone, as I am sure students of graphology (handwriting) will also be able to spot the fake! It is often easier to sound convincing verbally without being seen than it is by also being on view. How many of us, when wishing to complain, or say something with which we feel uncomfortable for some reason, will opt to either write or telephone. People who especially wish to hide their true feelings may wish to type letters, often using computers so that the words can be finely tuned before the letter is sent.

In order to appear successful and to be accepted by others, we may set out to create an image and to react in a way best suited to our ultimate goals, but our dress and grooming must also reflect this image, as otherwise a conflicting message may be sent out. There is a lot to learn about appearance, so let's start to look a little more deeply at what we may already know and accept about it.

Does appearance play a part?

When people meet us, their first impression is usually based on what we look like. By that, I don't just mean our height, weight, colouring etc., as all these can be altered with shoes, dress styles, diets, hair dyes, contact lenses, cosmetics, etc. I also mean our clothing. Although obviously there is a lot more to a personality than outward appearance and what jobs and interests they have. We do tend to judge the general type of personality someone has by the clothing they wear. Those people who wear jogging suits, trainers and so on a lot will probably be judged to be sporty types. Those people who wear a leather jacket, leather gloves, jeans and high leather boots will probably be judged to be interested in motorcyles, or even active motorcylists. Likewise, we will be able to spot the businessman by his suit. By the appearance of someone, we will be able to instantly decide (albeit sometimes mistakenly), whether they are the sort of people we would feel comfortable with, as we may already have formed an idea of their social status, their interests and even perhaps their occupation by their clothing.

In business situations, we often have the opportunity to speak to people on the telephone before we arrange a meeting. We will very probably have already made an informed judgement on a person before we even meet them based on their voice, the way they speak and what they say. However, when we get to shake hands with them for the first time, this may change or be refined because we have made a further judgement, based on what they look like. Even though we may have spoken to them on the telephone and made a

mental impression of the sort of person they are, we take more note when we meet them. In fact, it is thought that we initially make up our minds on people within the first seven seconds of meeting, based on appearance alone. (Neneh Cherry and Yousson N'Dour's song *7 Seconds* is about this.) A more complete opinion (in fact up to 90 per cent of the overall opinion) is made within the first 90 seconds, and takes into account stance, posture, gestures, appearance and speech. Those people who have ever been out on what is called a 'blind date' will be more than aware that we can create a totally wrong mental picture about someone from their voice, and find that someone they previously thought attractive, once seen, is someone who is far from attractive to us. We will discuss attraction and romance in depth in Chapter 3.

People often stereotype others by their hair colour and general appearance. It is said that people who wear glasses are often thought to be more intelligent than those who don't, that someone who wears a lot of makeup or whose hair is bleached blonde is likely to be less intelligent or even morally loose. Likewise, some

people consider that moustaches will make them appear older and that men with beards are likely to be independent minded. Many men, however, grow beards to hide what they consider to be a weak chin, whilst someone with a goatee beard may be trying to suggest their artistic or intellectual nature. It is interesting to note that, in Roman times, those with beards and moustaches were thought to be uncultured barbarians! It is said that blonde women are more fun to be with, whilst others would suggest that those who lighten their hair considerably are seeking attention. Unfortunately, it is generally considered that fair-haired men are less mature, and men with red hair are considered 'bad risks' being thought of as bad-tempered and generally unpleasant. On the other hand, women with auburn hair are thought of as high spirited and passionate, and similarly black hair is thought to indicate a sensual, energetic person. Generally, dark haired people are said to be more mature, stable, serious, sensitive and intelligent than their lighter haired counterparts.

Similarly, people also tend to judge someone's facial appearance, or even head size and make snap judgements on the sort of person they are. A small head is considered to be a sign of a restless, changeable person, a person with an egg shaped or oval head is considered the idealist, the intellectual (hence the term egg-head for academics), whilst a large head has always been considered to be a sign of leadership, nobility and intelligence – hence possibly the reason why many political, religious and royal persons accentuate their head size by wearing a symbolic head-dress, crown or hat. Teeth also play a part in our initial assessment of a person. Studies in the USA have shown, for example, that 85 per cent of adults feel that ugly or crooked teeth have been a handicap in their social and working lives, and likewise many people feel that damaged or blackened teeth are undesirable characteristics. People with white, healthy teeth are assumed to be people who look after themselves, (or it is fair to say people who have good dentists) and it is said that those with neglected teeth are likely to be unselfconscious people, concerned with things other than appearance.

Lips are also taken into account when we judge appearances. People with thin lips are considered generally to be mean, inhibited

or even vengeful, whilst those with full lips are often considered to be generous, sensual and happy. Downturned lips, as well as being a sign of a pessimistic nature may also be considered to show obstinacy, whilst upturned lips are halfway towards a smile, and are considered to be the sign of an outgoing personality.

What can we do to make ourselves seem more attractive? We can alter our image by our clothing, concentrating on certain styles and colours.

We all have our own likes and dislikes. We all have colours which we like to wear, styles which we feel happy with, and clothing which we reserve for important occasions. It is true to say that our clothing can not only give indications about our personality, but can also indicate our financial status. People on limited incomes or tight budgets are not able to afford the luxury of expensive clothing. Clothing companies who allow payment over weeks and charity shops selling second hand or slightly damaged clothing are often frequented by those who have tight budgets and are on the look out for a bargain, and it is also fair to say that many shops do a huge trade when the sales are on, because we want to look nice and in our modern world, that often costs us!

We are all conscious of our appearance, and most of the time want to create the right impression, especially when meeting people for the first time. It is said that body image increases during adolescence, and that most people, when asked to describe themselves, will concentrate on talking about their appearance rather than on what sort of person they are. In effect, appearance has little relation to actual personality, and most students of behaviour will agree that too much emphasis is placed on the effect of appearance on personality.

Most people, however, will be aware of the term 'power dressing'. This is something done to create an impression, usually of being in control, being confident. In business situations, the way we dress can often have a make-or-break effect on whether we succeed. If you are going for a job interview, you want to create the right impression and may spend a lot of time deciding what to wear, and we will talk about dress at work later. We will discuss improving business relationships and dressing for business in Chapter 5.

It is a fact of modern life that much emphasis (some would say too much emphasis) is placed on outward appearance, from the weight we are, to our hairstyle, clothing, our race, overall grooming, our smell – the list goes on. Sad that it is to admit, society often takes more notice of the appearance of a person than on what they are inwardly, what sort of person they really are, and a great deal of unhappiness can result if a person feels that they don't conform to what are seen to be 'accepted standards of appearance'. This is a sad indictment on the world at large, but it is unfortunately true that we take a great deal of notice of appearance, and make judgements based on this.

What some people consider attractive isn't what others may think, but it is fair to say that attractiveness isn't just based on appearance, but on speech, behaviour and conduct. Incorrect, bad or inappropriate conduct can make even a physically attractive person appear ugly, and being attractive is far more than what we wear. It is also about who and what we are. It is about being happy with our appearance, making the best of what nature bestows and not futilely searching for unreachable goals.

What we wear and the way we wear it makes a statement about us. Fashion trends come and go, and often we feel compelled to follow the trends set, or sometimes even deliberately seek to create an image which is really not the true 'us'.

Many times, in order to create the right impression, we will wear something out of the ordinary. I remember a few years ago, wishing to create a more feminine appearance when going out for a meal to somewhere swish with a male friend from work. He'd said that he viewed me as a 'mate' and didn't see me as a woman, and admitted that he failed to think of my emotional side. I was upset by this, and so spent a lot of money hiring an expensive gown. It was in a shade of lilac which I felt comfortable with, but it had a plunging neckline which made me feel decidedly uncomfortable. I was told I looked stunning, and comments were passed about the femininity of my dress (so the effort paid off), but I felt totally uncomfortable all evening because I was dressed in a way which was not natural for me. This little exercise is, however, something we can all do. We can all wear something a little different and see what effect this has on

those around us. If we always wear a suit at work, people who meet us in our jeans away from work may have a totally different opinion about us. They will react differently. From this information, you can decide on different styles of dress for different occasions. You can also see how confident you feel in different clothes. Try wearing different clothes to work and see how people respond. Likewise, try approaching strangers (pretend you are looking for a certain shop in town) and see how they react to you in a series of different types of clothing. You will then see, first hand, how we all tend to categorise people by their appearance, and you can use this information for future occasions.

When I first started work in the mid 1970s, the company I worked for would not allow ladies to wear trousers for work. It was considered an inappropriate image for the company (I worked for a firm of estate agents). I remember we had a temp come to work with us once, and she was sent home for coming to work in what I considered a very smart pair of trousers, even though it was mid-winter and trousers were obviously warmer. What we wear at work can send out messages about ourselves, and our employers, and for this reason, many people in banks and building societies, as well as supermarkets and shops, now have uniforms. It is considered to be a fact that people will take more seriously those who are dressed in a smart and professional way.

We all make judgements on people based on their appearance, but we can also look past the clothing and look at the person's physical characteristics to make such judgements. Some may say that we subconsciously associate the tall and slim in this world with success and competence, for example.

We can also learn much about a person from their environmental appearance – their home, car, etc. You can tell what they feel to be important in their lives, what type of people they are (tidy or not), and also how they relate to others within the security of their own environment.

In much the same way as we can power dress, we can also place furniture and ourselves in certain positions to create power and control over others within the room, but more of that later too!

If you are seeking to improve your image, become more attractive, I would suggest that you seek the advice of your family members. How do they see you? How does this relate to how you see yourself? You might also wish to record yourself and watch the video to see how you looked, behaved, etc., in a variety of differing situations. Try to look past the event that is being recorded, the memories it brings back, and take an objective look at yourself. Have a look at your wardrobe. Look at the sort of clothing you have, its condition, its colour, its style. If you feel a revamp is necessary, you might think about obtaining some help. Women with long hair often look totally different with their hair in a shorter style, or curled instead of straight, or a different colour. Talk to your hairdresser, get a few suggestions first. Look at magazines showing fashion, watch television fashion shows and copy what you see. Look at what is considered fashionable, what colours are in vogue and, especially if you are on a tight budget, consider looking around at charity shops and sales to see what you can pick up. At the end of the day, however, it is important to realise your limitations, and that includes age. Remember that we can often become an object of ridicule if we dress in fashions more suited to younger people.

From a body language angle, try to smile as much as you can, and develop a genuine smile, rather than a fake smile where the eyes don't seem to fit into the equation. Try to be friendly, to give a lot of eye contact, as people respond better to people who look at them – it conveys interest. As we will see as we progress, we also need to be open in our posture, open with our gestures, and learn how to move into someone's personal space without appearing to be an invader or threat. Leaning forwards towards people can help to do this. Remember that you must listen to other people as much as you must talk with them.

When we meet people, we might notice that they use a lot of hand movements in conversation. This is something you can observe even from a distance, and it is really a very interesting exercise to watch people in conversation and take note of their hands. We are now going to start actually looking at body language, and will start with the hands, as it is something you can easily observe, anywhere, any place and any time. You don't have to know the people you are

watching – all you have to do is watch. You might try, even at this early stage, to record something from the television, turn off the volume, and watch the hand gestures. It is obviously better if you record something with conversation – chat shows, comedy routines, sit-coms, soaps and so on, as you will then get a chance of observing some hand movements. Try to divide the programmes you tape into actual situations versus acting, and see if you can spot any differences. You can then even start to decide whether acting really is true to life!

What do our hands say?

Our hands tell a lot about us, and I'm not referring to what someone who studies palmistry might tell us. I am talking about the way we use our hands.

It is generally accepted that the French, Italians and Greeks use their hands in conversation far more than other races. You can tell a lot about somebody just by observing what they do with their hands. We shake hands, hold hands, guide and touch with hands to show concern or understanding, we may use our hands to indicate speed, the size of an object, but we also wave hands when leaving, and move our hands in other ways, such as touching our nose, stroking our chin, scratching our head, rubbing our palms together, clapping, and so on, all of which indicate a variety of different meanings. In this next section, we will start to look a little more deeply at the sorts of things we do with our hands, and learn the meanings behind these. This is by no means an exhaustive list of signals, and further study and research is recommended. You may wish to try *Teach Yourself Body Language*, also published by Hodder and Stoughton.

Please remember, DO NOT TAKE THESE SIGNS IN ISOLATION, AS ON THEIR OWN, THEY MAY BE MISINTERPRETED. LOOK FOR CLUSTERS OF SIGNALS IN READING MEANING.

Handshakes – Many nationalities will shake hands on meeting, although the customs for handshakes may vary slightly with different nationalities. Many French will shake hands both on entering and leaving a room, much as can be said in the case of business meetings, where a deal is being closed. What is common, however, is the distance kept between the two parties. In Western culture, men will often wish to keep their arms at full stretch, in order to maintain the required space between them, circumstances permitting. We will talk about zoning and personal space in Chapter 2.

It is unusual for people who know each other well, or who are close to handshake. Close friends or family may hug each other, and so might those wishing to put us at ease or show concern, who might go as far as holding both our hands. This should not be confused with what is termed the *politician's handshake*, where the extended hand will be held in the handshake whilst the other hand of the 'politician' will be placed over the gripped hand.

In some countries, it is considered strange for male family members to hug, and so you could well see son and father, two brothers, or other such relatives within a family shake hands on meeting or on leaving. Usually, however, this handshake will be accompanied by touching the other person's right forearm or right shoulder with the left hand, showing the closeness of the relationship.

It is originally thought that the handshake came about to show to the other person that there were no concealed weapons up the sleeve, and also to indicate, by the open hand, that friendship and honesty were being offered. If you think back in history, many civilisations used their hands to show honesty. The Romans, for example, would put their hand against their chest, whilst the American Indians would raise their open hand towards the sky.

Much can be gauged by the sort of handshake given, but taking handshakes in isolation is a dangerous pastime. Some people will offer a firm handshake, which may seem to indicate firmness of purpose and strength of character. Other people will seem quite weak in their handshake, and we may feel as a result that this is a weak character, someone less effective and strong, especially if we are talking about men. However, it is worthwhile bearing in mind

that artists, musicians and those who work with their hands, like surgeons, can also offer a weak handshake, based on fear of damage to their hands, which are a vital part of their working lives. So again, don't jump to conclusions.

We must all of us, at some time or another, have come across the clammy handshake. This is generally a good sign of nervousness, as the palm will sweat when we are nervous, but you should also take into account the room temperature and the weight of the individual, as people who are overweight may sweat more than thinner colleagues, and obviously we all sweat in hot temperatures, especially if we have been rushing about. There are various zones we occupy when we handshake also, and these will be discussed in the next chapter, when we take a look at our personal space.

Holding your hands/arms behind you – There are many people who walk with their hands behind their backs, with one hand lightly clasping the other hand. Many who have been in the military do this as a matter of course, as do many policemen, politicians and other people who are authority figures within society. This indicates someone who feels they are superior, or who is extremely confident with themselves, their station in life and their position with regards to those in whose company they find themselves. As the body is open to attack, as it were, it shows a lack of fear and supreme confidence. Generally, this sort of gesture is accompanied by a chin-held-high stance, and is not confined to men, but crosses the genders. Should **one hand be gripping the wrist of the other**, this is a sign of an attempt at confidence, which is not exactly the case. There is a frustration here, a lack of self-control, and the person concerned is trying hard to seem relaxed. Generally this stance is adopted whilst standing, and is often also accompanied by scratching of the head or pulling at the collar. You should look to see how tightly the hand is clenched, and how tightly the other hand grips the wrist or arm. This is a similar gesture to what is known as the *locked ankles gesture*, and is generally done by people who are angry, frustrated, stressed, anxious or concerned, but who wish to some degree to hide this – putting their hands behind them, out of view of someone facing them, does just this. If the hands are held quite high behind the back, this indicates timidity. Should the hand

be moved even further up the arm, however, this shows even more tension and nervousness, as if one hand is trying to hold back the other. It is naturally a difficult and uncomfortable position, as you will see for yourself if you try it.

Crossing your arms in front of you – This generally indicates someone who is protective of themselves, preoccupied or self-absorbed. It is also a defensive mechanism, a tense position. Nothing and nobody can get at our hearts when our arms are held across ourselves. Studies suggest that women who sit with their arms folded across their chest are giving out signals of indifference or downright dislike of someone else.

Clenching hands – If someone is holding a conversation and has their hands clenched, this is a sign of anger, or that the person concerned is apprehensive and finds the conversation painful or frustrating and is holding back from doing or saying something. This is something often observed by people sitting in a chair, at which point in time their ankles are also likely to be locked or crossed. Women tend to have ankles crossed close to their body, whilst men will have their ankles crossed in front of them. **Clenched fists** are one step further, showing anger or threat. A good tip here is to look at whether the hands are so tightly clenched that the skin is beginning to turn white. Hands can be clenched in various positions – if the person concerned is sitting at a desk, for example, they may be clenching their hands in front of themselves around chin level, or in another raised position. They may rest their clenched hands on the desk, or conversely, if standing they may clench their hands together in front of them and at a relatively low level. Current studies suggest that the height of the clenched hands denote varying levels of frustration, with the higher the hands, the more negative the attitude. It is currently suggested that clenched fists take us back to our cavemen ancestors, when it was obvious that a clenched fist meant someone was likely to be struck or hit, and it is also noted that women seldom clench their fists whilst talking, it being seen subconsciously at least as a masculine thing. It has been suggested that, in business situations, those who sit with their hands clenched are unlikely to have success in negotations, as people find difficulty in relating to those whose hands are not open, especially in business situations, as it is subconsciously registered that they are under stress. In certain European countries, a clenched fist at the end of a bent and upward moving arm is an insult, and this is something that you may see in cases of road rage. In Japan, however, a fist punched lightly in the stomach area indicates the concept of suicide, reflective of the use of the knife. **Drumming the fingers** on a desk or table top may also indicate stress, frustration or anxiety, or someone who is trying to deceive. It can also indicate boredom, and often in business situations, you will see someone doing this, indicating that they feel frustrated that the conversation is continuing and wish to get on with other things.

Steepling – When the fingertips and thumbs are pressed together, the person is confident of their opinion, feeling that they are superior to the person or people to whom they are talking. They are in control, smug about their opinions, even proud or egotistical. This hand gesture is called steepling because it to some degree is similar to the steeple of a church. The finger tips are joined together, and the result is a steeple-type effect. Should the head of the person concerned be tilted back at the same time, with the nose in the air, this indicates arrogance or at the very least supreme self-confidence, and it is usual to see steepling in people such as clergymen, lawyers and business executives, or in a business setting, this is often the position someone will give just prior to giving a lecture and pontificating on 'how I see the situation'. As with clenched hands, there are various positions to consider. Sometimes, a person sitting at a desk will have their elbows on the desk and steeple upwards. Other times, especially if there is no desk there, the person will have

their steepling at a lower angle. Again, the higher the steepling display, the more confident the person is of what is being said, whilst the lower steeple is indicating that the person still feels in control but may be listening to a counter-argument or considering a previously made point in more depth. Women generally use the lower or covert type of steepling. Another form of steepling, known as subtle steepling, is made when the hands are joined more closely together, perhaps with one hand seeming to cup over the other. The meaning of authority is, however, constant. Steepling should not be confused with **hands pressed together as if in prayer**, which indicates a need to persuade, or underline a point previously made. Having said that, I said this recently to a friend of mine who was about to eat a bowl of soup, and he told me that he wasn't trying to persuade me of anything. He was merely trying to warm up the pat of butter he had in his hands which he intended to use on the roll that had come with the soup!

Hands clasped back of neck or head – This is a sign of danger, as the person concerned is desperately trying to control his or her anger or annoyance, which cannot be expressed openly. If, however, the head appears to be resting on the hand, or even on a thumb, boredom is indicated, and the person is just stretching out, waiting for the situation to end. To make sure which applies, look for facial expression, where the eyes are pointing and whether the face is flushed with annoyance.

Both hands behind the head – This shows a feeling of superiority or arrogance, and is usually accompanied by a leaning backwards with elbows pointing outwards. This is someone who feels they are in control, and is a gesture which seems to have crossed over the Atlantic from America, where it is far more common. However, if **one hand is put behind the head** and the neck rubbed, this indicates frustration, anger and annoyance. This is a defensive gesture, and often it really does mean that somebody is being 'a pain in the neck'.

Rubbing palms together – This is all about expectancy, and can mean excitement if the hands are rubbed together quickly, and that the person concerned is really happy about the outcome of something – this is the 'let's get on with it' gesture. The speed at

which the palms are rubbed together is more important to notice, as it gives an indication of the intent of the person concerned. A business person for example who rubs her hands together quickly when talking to a client, is showing that she is thinking of them and their happiness, as opposed to someone who is trying to pull the wool over the other's eyes, which is indicated if the rubbing is very slow. Obviously it is worthwhile remembering that some people might just be rubbing their hands together because they are cold, and likewise in business discussions between partners, rubbing the hands together may well indicate a feeling that there is a lot of money to be made! Similarly, someone who is seen to be rubbing their palms against their clothing are showing that their palms are likely to be damp, and this could indicate nervousness, or again that they are just overly hot.

Wringing hands – This is another version of clenched hands, and is often seen when a person feels in a position of having to defend themselves, are tense and feeling concerned, unsure of what the next step should be.

Crossed first and middle fingers – Is a common sign which normally indicates someone who is saying 'I hope so' or who is relying on luck. Researchers suggest that this gesture stems from a magic defence against evil attack, whilst in some countries, especially in Latin America, this gesture is done to indicate two people who are very close to each other as in 'we are really as close as that', whilst in Turkey, crossing fingers indicates the breaking up of a friendship or relationship.

Often during the course of conversation, we bring our hands in contact with other parts of the body, especially the face, and we are now going to look at some of these gestures and see what they mean. Often these gestures are quite refined, but usually, hand to face gestures indicate negativity, doubt, and even deceit and lying. However, as always it is important that we look at all the signs together, rather than taking things in isolation.

Hand resting lightly on the cheek – This indicates the person is analysing and taking in what is being said – you only have to think of Rodin's sculpture entitled *The Thinker*, to realise that this has

been known for centuries. If they have their index finger pointing upwards, this suggests a negative reaction to what is being said, especially if they are leaning forward toward the speaker.

Rubbing, stroking or touching the nose – Indicates that the person is not sure and is having a few negative thoughts. This is a variation of the hand to mouth gesture, which we will discuss shortly, and could indicate someone is lying, although it could also indicate someone has an itchy nose! I remember once seeing a video of someone who was talking to his wife, trying to convince her that he wasn't having the affair that she suspected him of having. He couldn't look her in the eyes, avoided her eye contact as much as possible, and actually turned his body away from her, as if he felt unable to face her. He also repeatedly rubbed his nose, and, looking downward towards the floor, exclaimed that he wasn't having an affair, and he was really just a friend to the lady in question. This all indicated that he wasn't speaking the truth. **Touching the eye** is another sign of possible deceit, but again should not be taken in isolation.

Those people who are being subjected to a sales pitch will often be seen rubbing below the nose, to indicate that they feel a con-trick is being tried on them – they 'smell a rat'. Should they then begin to feel a little less apprehensive about what is being said, they may **put their hand to their chin and stroke it**. This indicates they are thinking carefully and considering the matter further, possibly being

about to make a decision. This is something sales people are often trained to watch, and they may then either home in on the sale or change tactics and start to be less aggressive in their sales pitch and appear more friendly. Sales people will also watch for things like someone sucking at the earpiece of their spectacles, as this is another sign that considerable thought is being given to the subject. If, however, the hand moves to actually **cup the head**, a gesture often seen when people are sitting around a table, this indicates boredom and can be often observed in business meetings, more of which later. The eyes will probably be looking downwards, the glance will not waver, and the person may even seem to be staring blankly at nothing, the chin will also drop, and there is a possibility, especially if a pen and paper are handy, that the person concerned will also start to doodle. If the **hand is on the cheek, the finger closed, but the index finger is pointing upwards**, this indicates someone taking an interest in what is being said. You may also see people alter this gesture slightly by moving their **thumb under the chin, bending the fingers around the mouth and the index finger pointing upwards**. This is a sign of someone having a few doubts about what is being said to them, and possibly making a critical evaluation. When feeling sad or unhappy, we may also put our **hand to our face and cup it**, especially when sitting in a chair or behind a desk, as if the hand is comforting us. It will be obvious to all around us that we are unhappy as the eyes may be focused downwards and the corners of the mouth be turned down, showing everyone how unhappy we really are.

Tapping the nose with one finger, usually the forefinger, is normally a sign, in British circles especially, of confidentiality, secrecy or complicity, especially if the tap is on the side of the nose. Moving your hand up to tap the front of your nose, however, indicates that you wish someone to keep their nose out of your business. Rubbing under the nose generally indicates that you feel uncomfortable, and is something that is done more often when we are lying than at any other time. If, however, the hand is held under the nose for a time whilst listening, we are likely to be thinking seriously about a problem.

When observing people, you will see that many, whilst talking, are **moving their hands about**. Some nationalities would seem to do

this more than others, but we all move our hands about when we are talking. Try asking someone to explain something to you, say what they do for a living or what they did last week, and you will notice that everybody moves their hands around. Normally, if talking of something concerning the future, a person will automatically gesture to the right with the right hand and move the left hand towards the right. That is because we normally see the future as being somewhere over in one direction, usually to the right or way in front. Talking about things relating to the past normally sees people gesture towards the left or even behind themselves, whilst present things show up with gestures which are in front of us as we speak. Gestures can speed up, slow down, and remain constant, but the speed at which movements are made will show whether there's tension, excitement or pleasure being described.

Rubbing the ear or pulling the ear lobe – This shows someone who is not really interested in what is being said, and wishes to block out the words, or who is politely waiting for an opportunity to get a word in. As we can speak at anything up to 700 words per minute, those people who are waiting to interrupt often have to use such signals to let us know that they wish to speak, especially if the conversation is being held by someone who is anxious and needs to 'spill the beans'. Should the **finger be put in the ear**, they have heard enough, or want to speak themselves; likewise they may actually **pull the earlobe forward over the ear** to indicate that they have heard enough. This may also be accompanied by **one hand coming forward** to indicate stop.

Scratching can indicate either lies and deceit or a feeling of uncertainty, but do remember that scratching can be done just to relieve an itch.

Lightly scratching the side of the neck with either one or two fingers – If the person doing this is actually speaking at the time, this indicates they are being insincere or lying, or that they themselves are not convinced of what they are saying. You may notice this with public speakers who are giving a talk based on written material which is not their own, or with which they generally feel uncomfortable. If the listener is displaying this gesture, he or she feels that the person talking is being insincere or lying or feels

uncertain about whether they agree with what is being said. Studies suggest that most people scratch about five times.

Scratching the head – This shows someone is perplexed, doubtful and uncertain. It could, of course, also indicate that someone is unhappy with their hair, their head itches or they feel generally uncomfortable.

Rubbing the eye, eyes lowered and eyebrows raised in disbelief position – This is the classic deceipt cluster. The eyes are lowered, or sometimes even closed, to block out the deceit and avoid eye contact which could give the game away, although rubbing the eye, as an isolated gesture, indicates doubt.

Covering the mouth with the hand – This is usually something which indicates that the person speaking isn't telling the truth. You only have to watch children to see this gesture, and parents will then immediately know that their child is hiding something. This can also be accompanied by a clearing of the throat, or fake cough. This gesture shouldn't be confused with those whispering, who also cover their mouths, and who will also move closer to the listener, possibly to as near as 15 cm (6 inches) away. Should a person be covering his mouth with his hand whilst listening to others, he is either shocked by what they said, which will be obvious by other facial signs and perhaps verbal communication, or he feels that you are lying. Sometimes, a person will be halfway through a sentence and then put their hand to their mouth. This usually means they have let something slip and wished they hadn't said something – it is as if they are wishing they could take the words and put them back into their mouths. Speaking out of the side of the mouth is an extension of the covering the mouth with the hand gesture, indicating that it is necessary to be seen to be hiding the conversation.

I used to know someone who regularly put his hand to his mouth when he spoke, but that was because he was unhappy about his teeth, and wished to cover them over with his hand. Once he had resolved the problem with his teeth, it took him some time to get out of the habit of covering his mouth with his hand when he spoke. I am mentioning this at this point as it serves to underline the need to take into account other signs and existing knowledge of the person

concerned, where this is appropriate. Likewise, we may put our hands to our mouths to stifle a yawn, disguise a hiccup or when we are coughing. Sometimes, a person sitting behind a table or desk may put **both hands in front of their mouth**, generally in a sort of collapsed steepling, and continue holding the gesture throughout the whole of a discussion, both when she is speaking and when she is listening. When listening, she may actually touch her lips with her closed fingers. This is normally someone who is waiting for the right opportunity to open up, at which point the hands will move away from the mouth and the tone of the conversation may change.

When angry or exceptionally frustrated, a person may be seen **pulling the collar away from the neck**. This indicates that they are possibly lying, or that they feel they need to let off steam. It is said that when we lie, a tingling feeling is often felt around the face and neck, and we feel the need to either scratch it or relieve it by pulling at our clothing. Again, it is worthwhile also taking into account environmental factors, the heat in the room and the season of the year before taking such things in isolation.

If being questioned, and feeling it necessary to defend one's honesty, reputation and character, we naturally tend to **put our hands to our chest**, indicating that we are being sincere and honest. You are subconsciously putting your hand near to your heart, and are signalling that you are speaking from the heart. This gesture can be done by either both hands being used, or just one, and will be accompanied by speech indicating that we are being truthful. As we have already said, this sort of gesture was often used by Roman soldiers, as a salute of loyalty and honesty, and a similar gesture is still used by American people when they pledge allegiance to the flag.

We also use our hands to point, and sometimes even use our thumbs.

Pointing a finger, especially the index finger, at an individual or group signifies dominance, aggression, anger and authoritarianism, and is often accompanied by strong verbal indications. However, it is obviously also something we do when we are pointing out someone to a stranger, or giving directions. Most of us will react

badly if someone points a finger at us, and either turn away or at least become defensive, and in arguments, it is relatively common to see people pointing fingers at each other, as likewise it is quite common to see people repremanding either children or animals by pointing or wagging their fingers at them. Nothing is ever gained by using this gesture with adults. Often it just arouses anger, as it can take us back to childhood situations, and we will automatically feel that the person doing the pointing is trying to indicate that we are being childish, becoming dominant or aggressive, or both.

We also should take account of the **thumbs**, which are important in their own right, and are often used by those people who already feel superior. Lawyers, for example, and those making speeches, may often hold on to their waistcoat with their fingers folded round it and their thumb displayed in an upward position. This shows they are in charge. Likewise, we may all put our **thumbs up** to indicate that we are feeling happy, successful, confident and well. It is thought that we all inwardly know that the thumb indicates superiority, and may seek to hide our feelings of such by putting our **hands in our pockets**. However, you may notice as you look around, that many people will have their **thumbs protruding from the pockets**, even though the hands may be hidden. Again dominance is suggested. Should someone be standing or sitting with their **thumbs in their pockets or wrapped behind a belt**, with their fingers openly pointing towards their crotch area, this is a two fold signal. Should the person be a man talking to a women, this is an overtly sexual sign, whereas should the man be talking with another man, this is a signal of aggression.

Hands in pockets indicates we feel the need for comfort. You may also notice men, especially, playing with their change. Again this indicates a degree of nerves and that the person concerned is seeking comfort or an outlet for their nerves.

Putting hands on hips is an aggressive and threatening stance. It also indicates a degree of readiness for action, especially in situations which feel uncomfortable. Women tend to put their hands on their hips to accentuate their body lines, and thus this becomes quite a sexual stance.

We sometimes also have **our arms folded, thumbs pointing upwards**, which should not be confused with the look of dejection we have already discussed. Both superiority and defensiveness are being indicated here. Arms folded usually indicates either a defensiveness and protectiveness of ourselves or a negative attitude – we often fold our arms when bored, feeling defensive, as has already been noted, and it is said from current studies that folding our arms is the most common gesture worldwide. It is also said that this stance can influence the behaviour of others, as one person in a group with arms folded will influence others within the group to mirror the stance. In fact, it is quite interesting to watch groups of people and see how people mirror image the gestures and stances of those around them, especially if they are friends and feel comfortable with the group. With the thumbs pointing upwards, the folded arm stance indicates someone who has made up their mind, and will be almost impossible to convince. We may also seek to **hide the thumbs inside the fist**. This demonstrates a difficulty in analysing a problem, whilst **jerking your thumb** toward someone is usually a signal of disrespect and intended ridicule – this is often seen when one person is talking to another about a third person – conversations like 'Well you know all about him, don't you.....' The thumb will be pointed over the shoulder of the person speaking, and are backwards glance over the shoulder may also be shown, even if the person being spoken about is nowhere within earshot.

Standing with both hands open and in front of us indicates sincerity, and is often used by those people who feel they have to defend themselves by explaining themselves a little more. Should this be accompanied by a **shoulder shrug**, the indication is that there is sincerity, but the person concerned really doesn't know what the other person expects them to do. They feel totally helpless in the situation and inadequate at getting their point to be accepted. Some experts call this open-handed gesture the **hand shrug**.

As I have already said, the above is really not an exhaustive list. There is a lot that we have not been able to cover here, and further study is well advised. However, you will have seen from what we have already discussed relating to hands that there really is a lot to learn and understand. Before we go a little further on to learn about

personal space, zoning and so on, we will have a few exercises you may wish to have a go at to see what you remember, what you pick up automatically and what you have learnt. All the answers will be found within the chapter we have covered, and it is up to you to decide for yourself how you have done.

PRACTICE

Pretend you are in a crowded room. There is somebody the other side of the room who you notice because they are on their own. This person is standing with head looking down, shoulders hunched over. They have their hands folded across their chest. They seem to be staring at nothing in particular. What would you assume from their body language to be their current state of mind?

You are going for an interview. Someone is already discussing matters in another room with the interviewer, and you are in the room with one other applicant. That person is sitting with ankles locked, and they appear to be gripping the arms of the chair. What would you assume about that person?

You are talking to a colleague at work about your recent holiday. They seem interested, are smiling and leaning forward, and are sitting with their hand on their cheek with index finger pointing upwards. As the conversation progresses, you notice that they are sitting completely still with their back against the chair, with shoulders rounded, and a blank expression. Their hand seems to be playing with one ear in a way they don't normally do, and when they see you looking at that, they pretend they are fiddling with their hair. What do you conclude?

Someone is walking along with their hands behind their back, one hand clasping the other. Their walk is upright, their head held high. They are wearing what seem to you to be expensive clothes in seasonal shades. Their shoes are sparkling and they walk at a relatively fast pace. Is this person happy, sad, authoritative, submissive, confident or lacking in self-esteem?

We walk into the boss's office to see her with hand on head, leaning towards the desk. The phone rings, she pushes her hand

through her hair, picks up the receiver and without speaking, bangs it straight down again with a sigh. As you walk in she looks at you and is about to speak. From these isolated comments on her body language, what would you expect her speech to reflect – anger, tension, happiness or sadness? Obviously, if we included the fact that her jaw was clenched and her shoulders hunched, we could home in on the possible answer!

Finally, remember, that if people feel they are being observed, they will most probably act differently, because they become self-conscious. In studies of non-verbal communication, this has been overcome by the use of two-way mirrors, so that the researcher can observe without being seen himself. Likewise, many studies are carried out using videotape, which has the advantage of being able to be viewed more than once, slowed down, speeded up and so on. One of the best ways to view people's body language is during idle chit-chat. When people are talking about things which are really not that important, you can mentally switch off from what they are saying and look more toward their body language. You might wish to try this sometime, but do try to listen a little!

2 PERSONAL SPACE

As you start to observe people a little more closely, you will notice that sometimes people stand several inches away from people they are talking to, and at other times they seem to stand really close. This is called zoning, and we all do it, whether we are conscious of it or not. In this chapter, we are going to start taking a look at how we stand in relation to other people, what happens when we 'invade' someone else's space, and then start to take a look at seating arrangements for the best possible conversation, how we use our body to point out our inner feelings and how important our stance and posture are.

The zones

We all need our personal space. Many of us, especially when standing in queues, will feel uncomfortable because the person behind us is standing a little bit too close.

Much of what we consider to be our own personal space depends on whether we grow up in crowded areas, as part of a large family, etc. City dwellers will tend to stand relatively close to each other when shaking hands and step forward to greet someone, whereas those from rural areas may stand further apart, and seem to lean towards one another when shaking hands, maintaining quite a distance. Likewise, where we stand in relation to others can have a social connotation – those in power will always wish to keep their distance from those who they consider lower in status.

There are four zoning groups depending on where we choose to stand:

The intimate zone – this is the zone of up to 45 cm (18 inches)
The casual zone – this is the zone of between 45 cm and 1.2 m (18 and 48 inches)
The social zone – this is the zone of 1.2 m to 3.6 m (4 feet to 12 feet)
The public zone – This is the zone of more than 3.6 m (over 12 feet)

It is worthwhile mentioning that women speaking with women tend to stand closer than men talking with men, or even men talking with women. Another point worthwhile noting is how we act towards people we consider subordinate. A waiter can stand for seemingly ages and be totally ignored, even though he is standing within a certain zone. This is what is commonly known as the non-person zone.

The intimate zone – this zone relates to close friends, those we love, as it allows us to more easily touch, hug or cuddle. This is by far the most important zone to look at when thinking in terms of loving relationships, and whether someone feels comfortable with you or not. This is really 'your space', and you will notice that when you feel attracted to someone or they feel attracted towards you, one or other of you will lean towards the other, moving into that 'personal space' without actually moving forward with the whole body. There is another division within this zone, which is from body contact to 15 cm (6 inches) away, and this is reserved solely for intimate relationships where you can observe lots of eye contact. Occasionally, someone may enter this zone to try to become 'more than friends'. This can cause us to feel threatened, and for this reason we should all be aware that even simply putting our arm on someone's shoulder, if we do not know them really well, could cause problems for that other person, even if we are merely trying to be friendly. People who stand too close or make too much eye contact with others may well find it difficult to make friends, for this reason, and learning all about body language and non-verbal communication can help them to ease into social interactions more successfully.

In crowds, many people invade our personal zone, and we accept less personal space than would otherwise have been the case, which most find uncomfortable. Unless we are exceptionally outgoing or feel attracted to the person sitting next to us, we will stare into space, cross our legs or our arms, read a book or magazine, avoid eye contact, maybe look away and remain totally impassive. This is because we feel uncomfortable, and we may also find ourselves staring at the ceiling. It is for this reason, experts suggest, that advertisers have realised the need to advertise on underground trains. Likewise, for this reason perhaps, in public areas we will all make our way to an area where nobody else is sitting, or sit at the end of the row.

The casual zone – this zone is the standard social zone, which allows us to talk comfortably with other people without feeling threatened. You will observe people standing in this zone at parties, at other such functions and at gatherings of people who know each other well as friends. Eye contact will be reduced, but still apparent, as will smiles, but their topic of conversation is more likely to be about the weather or some other impersonal subject, like work or general chit-chat.

The social zone – this zone is for strangers, including people who we are buying from, such as shopkeepers, as well as for people who may be working for us, such as a new employee or someone we have brought in to carry out a repair within the home. It is reserved for people we feel we do not know really well. Eye contact will be kept to a minimum, and conversation will be brief.

The public zone – this zone is the space we ideally need to be from an audience or crowd of other people we are addressing formally. Obviously, this public zone depends on the area available to us, as many of us, myself included, have held formal discussions and lectures with groups of people much closer to us than 3m (12 feet). Eye contact will rove around the group, focusing on individuals only briefly. Smiles will come and go, and the person giving the address will endeavour to be friendly, but from a distance. In the case of a nervous public speaker, the eye contact will seem to be towards the back of the room, permanently, so as to avoid much eye contact with those who are closer. It is a good technique to use at the start

of a lecture, as this will help the speaker lift their head and project their voice, as if speaking only to someone a distance away.

What signs indicate we have invaded someone's space?

There are various indications we can look for, some of which we have already mentioned in the comments made about cinemas and so on, but again these activities fall into four distinct categories:

Displacement activities – foot tapping, crossing and re-crossing legs, knee jerking, moving around in the seat to face another direction. If people have already turned away, you instinctively know that they wish no contact with you.

Eyes – not looking directly at the other person, closed eyes or frequently glancing away or in fact even turning away. Conversely, if you continue to look at a person, especially when they are talking to you, you will have a hard job to shut them up on occasions.

Defensive gestures – Crossing the arms to form a barrier between one person and the other, fiddling with jewellery, watch, bracelet, etc., through a feeling of frustration or anxiety, or resting the arm on the opposite leg when sitting down to create another barrier of protection.

Posture – Tensing up the shoulders by bringing them upwards towards the ears, lowering the chin to the chest, deliberately altering your stance so that it is totally the opposite to the other person. Leaning backwards in a chair is also a defensive, hostile and negative gesture, and when we are feeling uncomfortable, we also tend to stand on one foot, especially if in a group situation where we are feeling excluded from the conversation.

Looking at social seating

You can also learn a great deal from observing where people naturally sit in relation to someone else. Business executives, those engaged in counselling and those working within sales, the law and other such professions will all to some degree know how vitally important it is to place seats at the right angle to achieve the best results. In this section, we will take a look at seating in social settings, and where we should sit to our best advantage if we wish to engage in successful conversation.

Sitting directly opposite someone – As in the case of standing immediately opposite someone, when you have to sit looking at someone, it is often the case that we will inwardly feel threatened, under scrutiny, attack or interrogation – in fact, this is the seating position that many who employ interrogation techniques will choose, as you cannot look away, and if you also keep the proximity between interrogator and interrogatee small, or seek to move

towards the person under interrogation or put him or her in an armless chair, this will add to the feeling of discomfort and threat.

Sitting next to someone – In this position, if successful conversation is to take place, one or other of the people concerned, or possibly both, will have to shift round in their seats to attain any eye contact. As such, this is not a good seating position to adopt if you wish to engage in interesting and productive conversation, although if you are in a business discussion, sitting alongside someone is probably wise, as you are then indicating that you are in agreement with them and have similar aims. Likewise, those people in a close relationship will tend to sit next to each other, but in order to talk, will have to turn towards each other, lean towards each other and/or touch. Unfortunately, if people in groups tend to sit all next to each other, someone may feel excluded from the conversation. Put three people together on a sofa, for example, and the person in the middle will find it easy to talk to one or the other person sitting next to them, but the people at either end will not be able to converse.

Sitting slightly angled (in what is often termed the open triangular position) is by far the best way to sit if you wish to engage in conversation. Neither of the people will feel threatened if a certain distance between the chairs is allowed, and both will be able to view each other without feeling in competition or under threat. Space between the parties will be enough so that both can hear and observe, but not invade the other's personal space. This is the positioning of chairs which counsellors will employ when wishing to help someone with problems.

Sitting around a circular table is obviously a good idea for groups of people to be able to engage in conversation. Similarly, **standing in a circular group** will help to develop conversation, and this is something you will notice at parties especially.

how we sit

Sitting with **legs wide apart** is a very vulnerable position, and is also known as 'the crotch display'. Most of us, unless with friends or others with whom we feel comfortable, will wish to keep our genital areas protected and/or hidden, by closing or crossing the legs. By actually sitting with legs open, especially if you don't then put your hands in the open area to cover over the genital region, you are displaying confidence, and as such the thought that you feel yourself in charge. Women could also be indicating to any men in the area that they are available, so do watch this, unless you are actively seeking attention. You are also taking up a fair amount of space, thus making sure people keep their distance from you.

Sitting with one leg over the arm of a chair and the other leg on the floor shows a lack of concern, an easy going and relaxed attitude, feeling comfortable in the surroundings. Many children do this at home in much the same way as we might put
our feet on a table when sitting back in a chair. Again this is a

41

superiority, authoritative stance, and often shows someone with an indifferent attitude.

Sitting with **one leg under the other** is known as the **knee point** which suggests that you are in fact pointing the knee towards someone you find interesting. This position is a very relaxed way to sit unless, of course, you suffer with any arthritic problems, and makes for a relaxed conversation, because you are not sitting in a formal pose.

Straddling the back of the chair is a seating position most common to men. The back of the chair will then provide a barrier between the person and his audience, so that he is less open to any attack, and as such make him feel able to become more dominant or controlling. Likewise, a man who sits with one ankle crossed over the knee of the other leg (what is called the **leg lock** and thought to be a very American way of sitting), is really suggesting that not only does he feel superior, but that he is likely to wish to voice his opinion rather strongly. The higher the leg is crossed over the other, the more superior or aggressive the person is likely to be, as this is the sign of the competitor, the person who feels capable of arguing his point successfully. Should the person concerned also hold his arms on his leg, seeming to lock it into place, this is a person who has most definitely made up his mind, someone who is likely to be stubborn and unmoving. Sitting with legs crossed in this manner is a very masculine pose, and the only time you may see women sit like this is when they are wearing trousers and when they are feeling in total control.

Most of the time, men especially will sit in the more relaxed **legs crossed position** which is a defensive, protective gesture more adopted by the British and Europeans than other cultures. People also tend to stand with their legs crossed, when feeling defensive.

Normally, one leg will be slightly over the knee of the other, which will be tilted, creating a sideways sloping effect, with the toes of the upper foot relaxed. The **leg twine**, is very common for women, less common for men, is sitting with leg sloping over the other in a tilted way. Letting the shoe on the crossed leg drop or slip off at the back, indicates a relaxed attitude. If a women seeks to cover her knees,

generally speaking, she is signalling that she does not wish to be approached by any male in the group.

This leg position should not be confused with the **ankle lock or feet curled position** which is common to both sexes, and which indicates negativity, anxiety, anger, a wish to speak. Women are the only ones who, it would seem, tend to adopt the **foot lock position** when sitting. One foot is locked around the other leg, and this indicates a defensive attitude, as if one foot is seeking to protect the other. This stance will be repeatedly shifted, and the feet will unlock and lock again, and the person may also seem to wriggle around – again indicating a feeling of discomfort and wishing to leave.

Pointers to watch

We also tend to point our bodies, feet and legs towards people or areas, and this gesture, known as **pointing** is also something we must consider as a person's body and feet position indicates where they wish to go, whom they wish to talk to or are aiming their comments towards.

Should the two people be close friends, a couple, interested in each other from a romantic angle, or wishing to have a private conversation, they will face each other, with their **bodies pointing directly towards each other**. This effectively excludes other people from the conversation, in much the same way as sitting directly facing someone else.

When seated, we also tend to point our bodies and feet in the direction where our interest is held. When two people are sitting side by side, for example, you will find that one person is more likely to change his posture towards the other, and cross his or her legs to create a **knee point** towards the person they are talking with. Similarly, when in conversation, where the feet are pointing signifies the direction the person concerned would like to go, or conversely the person they are interested in. Most people will start off by standing with their feet either diagonally forwards in a neutral position or in a 'ten to two' clock position. As the conversation

moves and develops, the feet will shift, and start to point towards the person in the group that the individual finds most interesting, or most attractive in the case of mixed gender groups.

Should you ever attend a public meeting or lecture where the feet of the speaker can be observed, watch their stance. Watch to see how often the speaker points their foot towards a person or group of supporters or family. Subconsciously, the speaker may be seeking support, indicating their comments are addressed to that person or group, and mentally seeking perhaps to exclude the others as it is more comfortable. Their eyes may be looking around the room, taking in eye contact with others, but their feet will give them away.

Postural shifts

Posture changes depending on our emotions, the memories we are re-enacting, our conversation and our companions. When we were youngsters, most of us were told not to slouch, to sit up straight, and even to walk tall. The reasons behind all this were not only to avoid back problems, but also to ensure that we showed confidence, rather than low self-esteem by our stance. Standing straight and tall gives us an air of hopefulness and confidence and most people will notice us and take what we say with more readiness. Similarly, when we walk adopting an upright posture, with head held high and eyes focused forwards, we look far more confident and alert. We should aim for this sort of posture, a fairly brisk walking pace and a smile if we wish to be seen by others to be someone they wish to get to know.

Many physical changes in stance and posture relate not only to our ingrained habits, but also to our changing emotions. When we are angry, in addition to altering our facial expressions, our stance alters – we square our shoulders, tense ourselves, and seem to 'raise ourselves up to our full height'. When, however, we are feeling happy, full of energy and confident, our stance is more upright.

PRACTICE

During the course of this chapter we have concentrated our efforts on looking at space, seating, body stance, posture and how we use our limbs to indicate interest. We might now wish to start looking a little more at people with whom we have daily contact. Start to look at people, at their stance and mannerisms. Make a list of the qualities you feel they have, their attitude and general demeanor, and then match this up with various things you pick up from their body language. Obviously, on a day-to-day basis, their attitude could change as a result of circumstance, ill health or whatever. Do make sure that you take this into account, as we will all change, and our body language can alter quite dramatically, even within a short space of time, dependent upon what is happening to us at the time. People watching can be quite a fascinating experience, but do be careful not to stare at people. As we have already mentioned, people who feel they are under scrutiny will alter their body language because they feel threatened.

Given what we discussed in the previous chapter regarding appearance, you might also wish to make a note of how someone you know changes their body language when in different clothes, or in different settings where a change of image is necessary.

3 ROMANCE

In the course of this chapter, we are going to take a look at romance. You may already be in an existing, strong relationship. Conversely, you may be looking for romance, and unsure how to act in the company of someone you find attractive, finding yourself questioning whether they have any interest in you in a romantic way. You may come across someone you think is interested in you, merely to discover later that they are a notorious flirt. Could you have spotted the tell-tale signs?

Like attracts like

More often than not, we will find ourselves attracted to someone who has similar qualities to ourselves. It is true that we all want to be liked, and strangely most of us will also want to be liked by people that even we ourselves don't feel particularly warmly towards! We all have our 'types', and how many times do you hear people, especially on blind dates or first meetings say that 'so and so is really not my type'.

Some people are more **extrovert** than others, better in company, better at conversation, easily outgoing and relaxed with themselves. These people will generally be attracted to others who also feel at ease in company, rather than someone who appears to be shy and introverted, doesn't like to mix or who has difficulty in large groups of people. They will also feel attracted towards someone who physically is as attractive as they perceive themselves to be, however accurate this may be in truth. If we are somewhere on our

own (not for observation purposes as previously discussed but with the express desire of meeting new people) standing in a corner, straight faced, looking nowhere in particular, but possibly downwards, and possibly fiddling with a drink, we will give out the signal that we aren't interested in being approached.

We are more likely to be attracted to someone who smiles a lot. That, of course, is a two-way thing. If we feel anxious about a situation, we are unlikely to smile, and then other people may feel that we are unattractive and not wish to engage in conversation with us, even though we may feel drawn to them because they seem happy and relaxed because they are smiling.

People who are **introverted** need not necessarily be shy, but may appear somewhat unbending in stance, dislike being touched and avoid eye contact. You will spot those people immediately, but should you find them attractive be careful how you go, and be aware that this person will probably prefer being in less crowded areas when any initial contact is engaged. These are people who will respond better to quiet, both in voice and external noise.

Making contact

Eye contact is probably one of the most important early signs in getting to know someone new. You may have heard the old story 'our eyes met across a crowded room', but indeed this is often very true. We spot someone and endeavour to make eye contact with them without seeming to stare or draw too much attention to ourselves. We will look at them for a while, then look away, and then look again, spending more time looking at that person than is spent looking away. What we may also be doing mentally is taking a 'snapshot' of the person.

All that aside, we also need to **smile** when our eyes meet. Sometimes when we are nervous, we find it difficult to smile naturally and what we end up with is a fixed grin or conversely a nervous half-smile. If you feel really nervous, you might wish to try

practising a few quick smiles, as most of the initial attention given to you will be on your facial area and eyes, rather than on your body as a whole.

But how would you know if that person is interested in you? It is fair to say, at this stage, that there are always people who seem hard to get to know. All of us at some stage will have met people who we feel wary or uncomfortable with, people whose outlook on life, thoughts, feelings and general attitude do not gel with ours. It is always worthwhile remembering this, especially when trying to embark on a relationship, romantic or otherwise, and should you find it difficult to meet someone with whom you wish to share a romantic encounter, don't necessarily assume that the problem is theirs, and that they are difficult people to relate to – also remember to take a good look at yourself, how you present yourself, how you relate to others, what signals you are giving out.

Knowing whether interest is there

When someone is interested in you, not only will they smile at you and wish to make eye contact, but their facial colouring may change as the chemicals within the body react to show their interest, and their body posture will also tell of their interest. Even if they are on the other side of the room, you will be able to see that they are listening to you, they will possibly be leaning towards you or pointing their body or stance towards you in some way. You will be able to look at their feet and see whether their feet are pointing in your direction or indeed look at their stance to see whether they are turning towards you or not. If they are not interested, not only will their tone of voice indicate this, and sometimes this can be by a sharp retort, but you will also see how they react when you get close to them. When someone you feel attracted towards enters your personal zone, you will not feel threatened. If, however, someone you find unattractive enters your personal zone, you will automatically back off to recreate the space you need in order to feel comfortable.

Gestures to watch for

When we are interested in someone, we use specific body language to show ourselves off to our best advantage, or conversely to strike a pose which shows interest. These are called preening gestures or courting gestures, and we will start to take a look at some of these, dividing them off into gestures which women will tend to use, then gestures which men will tend to use.

Women's gestures – These fall into distinct categories, and which ones are followed seems to depend a great deal on natural characteristics. Some women will tend to smooth or play with their hair, whilst appearing to look downwards but head lifted, or smooth down their dresses, checking in any available mirrors that they are looking in order. Other more confident women will use overtly sexual moves, such as standing with hands on hips, legs open, to bring attention to their figures, moving their hips round in a sexual way, seeming to caress any bare flesh, especially legs. Sitting with legs crossed and hands folded around one knee is also a pose indicating interest, as is adjusting jewellery or even letting the tongue move around the lips to moisten them. Some women expose the wrist area, which when linked with the head toss is a show of interest. Every woman will feel she has a good feature, something that can be used, and will endeavour to use this to her advantage. For example, if she feels she has lovely hair, she will put her hand through her hair, long hair can be flicked back, she will use the light shining on her hair and so on.

Men's gestures – Men will often look as if they are on display, actively preening themselves. They will endeavour to stand erect and tall, maybe even breathe in if they feel their body may let them down, and straighten their ties, making sure their jacket is buttoned. They may hitch their thumbs around their belt with fingers pointing down towards their crotch, signalling that they are available, or as with women, stand with legs slightly wider than usual and hands on hips. Should he be sitting, he may well again widen his legs to give a crotch display, or turn to point in the general direction of the lady concerned with his foot.

SPOTTING THE FLIRT

People who flirt seem to follow the same guidelines as the rest of us, but to the extreme. These are the overly chatty people. These are the people with the raised laugh and the deeper, slightly louder voice, an extrovert person who will continue to maintain eye contact with another long after the rest of us would have looked away. They will seem to have confidence in abundance, and smile readily, easily and broadly.

Once contact has been definitely established, the practised flirt may well then seem to suspend interest, pull back, so that the other person now is not so sure that there was any initial interest, thus making them unsure in themselves and probably look more. The flirt may well then actually turn away, or create a barrier with legs or arms, but continue talking and then maybe turn back and smile. Once the interest is regained, the flirt will then initiate verbal contact. The walk towards the other party may seem accentuated, with chest pushed out. Women may roll their hips when they walk, whilst men may perhaps initiate a hands in belt stance, with fingers pointing towards the crotch area. He will seem very confident, and perhaps actually touch the other person concerned on the arm or shoulder, seemingly accidentally, or maybe as an obvious gesture. Any contact may be prolonged slightly longer than would normally be the case, and may also look the other person up and down. Should the contact be seen by the flirt to be cold, or should the initial interest seem to wain on introduction, the flirt will not prolong the contact, and they will move on to someone else and go through the whole ritual again.

It is worthwhile mentioning that we will all flirt to some degree, but practised flirts do everything in an exaggerated and more overt way than the rest of us.

WHAT THE EYES CAN TELL US

When we meet people, we tend to look towards their hands, facial expression and eyes, and we are now going to take some time to look at what the eyes tell us about someone else.

Obviously eyes help us to see but they also tell us how we react, and it has long been known by women that drawing attention to the eyes by using make-up is important, as you can seemingly increase the size of the eyes with make-up. Similarly you can draw attention to your eyes by choosing a striking coloured contact lens to ensure that people notice you. Whilst most people will find themselves attracted to large eyes, or eyes which are smiling, what we need to look at is **the pupils**. If we are to be successful in our use of body language, we need to learn to watch the size of pupils. When someone is interested in someone else, their pupils will enlarge or to be correct they will dilate, as if they are trying to take in more than previously. This is an emotional response over which we have no control. In times gone by, women in Italy especially, would put drops of belladonna into their eyes to cause enlarging of the pupils, but this is not recommended or used nowadays.

Eyes widen when we are angry, nostrils may flare, the jaw will appear set, and the eyebrows will lower into a frown. People who are nervous may find eye contact a problem, as will those who are telling a lie, plain disinterested, depressed or introverted, and all of us will naturally lower our gaze when talking about things which we find embarrassing or difficult.

We all move our eyes continually, both with people we feel attracted to and people we know in a broader sense. Nobody keeps their eyes focused on someone constantly. We may choose to sweep our gaze up and down their body once or twice, we may also look at various aspects of their face, focus briefly on one area then another, we will also look away to left or right to take a break.

People fall into two distinct categories – the lookers and the listeners. These studies suggest that when someone is looking upwards, he is thinking about something visual from the past, and is actually recalling this within his mind – he is a looker. If, however, the eyes seem to be glancing to the side, the person is recalling something audible, which could be a piece of music or a conversation from the past – she is a listener. Looking in one direction for a considerable time suggests that the person is thinking mainly in picture form and will be someone with a good imagination and a strong visual sense. This is the sort of person who will notice how things are wrapped, what people look like, what sort of clothes they are wearing, details about their appearance and so on. He or she will also be someone who concentrates a lot on this aspect of their own presentation. If someone has the tendancy to look sideways a lot, studies suggest that this is a person who thinks about things heard rather than things seen, and will be good at remembering conversations, sounds and so on. This person will, probably, also have a good sense of rhythm, and be less interested in what things look like, or what people look like, preferring to concentrate their attentions on what these people say and how they act. This may also reflect in their own personal dress sense.

If you perceive that the person you are with is someone who thinks in visual images, you would do well to describe things in great detail, in order for them to build up the mental picture in their minds. However, should the person be a listener, you can concentrate on what was said and relate that, rather than going into any greater detail about the circumstances, environment and so on.

Touching – is this advisable?

You may notice people being introduced or introducing themselves by offering their hand and wishing to shake hands – they are trying to make a personal contact. Much can be learnt from the handshake, but it shouldn't be taken in isolation as an indicator of

someone's personality and nature. We feel closer to someone we have touched rather than someone we haven't, and people who touch readily are more likely to have a positive attitude towards life generally than those for whom touching is a rarity.

Having engaged in eye contact, a smile exchanged, it is not unusual for someone to wish to open up a conversation and walk up to another person, hand extended, smiling and introduce themselves. It is not necessarily a good idea to be too touchy at the start of a new friendship, as it takes time to learn about the other person, and they may well not be of the touchy type. Some people are naturally touchy people though, and these normally emotional yet confident types are often really relaxed people, confident in company and with other people and also in themselves, and likely to be interested in clothes and textures, so can normally be spotted by their attire. It is worthwhile also pointing out that, as touchers, they may well also notice what you are wearing and touch your clothing to 'feel the texture'. Being a good listener is important in any interaction, as successful conversation demands that we listen to the other person, reply accordingly and really try to focus on what the other person is saying. Someone who nods all the time, looks away constantly, fiddles with things is obviously not that interested in what you are saying. You will know if someone is listening to you because they may well angle their head to the side a little, to show interest. At this stage, if you have received positive feedback, one or other person may wish to move closer, and if a person feels quite happy about someone moving closer to them, they should possibly just smile or at least pretend they hadn't noticed. Should the other person continually look away, yawn, smile quickly and not use much eye contact, the chances are that they are not really interested that much, and it is up to the individual how to end the contact.

SIX RULES FOR INITIATING GOOD CONTACT WITH PEOPLE

1 **Smiling** – Smiling is always a good indication of whether someone is friendly and open or not. When you smile at someone, you are saying that you have noticed them in a positive way. The person you are smiling at will register this, and take it as a compliment that you feel comfortable with them, and generally will smile back. If you then follow this through with some conversation, the feedback should be positive.

2 **Open posture** – Keeping arms and legs crossed creates a barrier, as does putting your hand across your mouth when speaking, which conveys that you have something to hide. When you are nervous, you may also move your hands around your face, and this is something that people will pick up on, and they in turn will tense. If you wish to make contact with people, and wish them to approach you, try to be within 1.75 m (5 feet) or so of that other person, so you are within approach distance. Remember – don't move too close too soon.

3 **Leaning forward** – This is another aspect of open posture, and shows interest in what the other person is saying. Leaning away from someone, especially if you then put your hands behind your head, gives them the impression that you find them and their conversation boring, disagreeable or alien to you in some way, and as such the other person will often then feel threatened, and the conversation will end.

4 **Touch** – Shaking hands is a good way of opening up a communication channel. With people we know well, obviously, a handshake would not be something we would consider. Remember that some people are very sensitive about being touched.

5 **Eye contact** – Together with a smile, eye contact and the maintaining of eye contact, is important in any form of communication. Remember to meet the other person's eyes from time to time, not all the time, and take in the whole of their face periodically. If you are shy, you may find that making and

maintaining eye contact is something you find difficult. If this is so, you might wish to try making eye contact for a couple of seconds at the most, and then smile.

6 **Facial and head movements** – Nod your head when you agree with something. Look interested. Remember to keep this going throughout the conversation, and change the angle of your head when the other person is speaking.

PRACTICE

Before we leave this chapter behind, let's see how much you have discovered.

John and Ruth are introduced at a party. The host is a close friend of Ruth's, and John is someone from work who the host feels would get on well with Ruth. When introduced, Ruth smiles quite happily, and the conversation seems to go well. John gets Ruth a couple of drinks and then feels that the relationship is going so well that he can take matters a stage further. What signs might he have picked up on which led him to this conclusion?

Brian and Denise are on opposite sides of a room at the local bar. Both are with other people, but neither is attached to anybody. What might an impartial observer look at to see whether there is any interest between Brian and Denise?

Susan starts a new job, and is told from the outset that Mick is the office flirt. What body language should she look out for to see for herself whether this is true or not?

4

FRIENDSHIP

In this chapter, we are going to take a look at friendship, in all its forms.

JUST BEING FRIENDS — WHAT IS A FRIEND?

Friends can be a rare commodity in the world we now live in, and it is fair to say that many people feel that they can count their real friends on the fingers of one hand.

Friendships are generally cultivated from amongst people who have similar interests, who are already known to us through family or secular associations, people of similar backgrounds or simple compatibility of personalities. The warm affection we feel for friends differs dramatically from romantic love. In fact there are many different types of deep affection. There is the affection we feel for friends; parents for their children; the passionate affection we may feel for a person of the opposite sex, as well as the love we may feel towards others who we don't really know. These various types of love: agape – unconditional love; philia – brotherly love; eros – romantic love, are all different. It is the philial type of affection to which we are referring when we talk about friends, and to be a friend to someone, you really should feel this philial affection, sentiment and feeling.

With friends, we have got over a lot of initial hurdles. Friends will, by and large, know a lot about us, know how we act and react in certain circumstances.

When we are with friends, we act and react differently from those with whom we have a romantic relationsip. When we know someone well, we can be ourselves, let our true feelings show through.

People who have really close friendships may know what the other person is going to say, nodding in agreement almost as soon as the sentence is started, smiling easily and openly, being relaxed in stance and posture.

We tend to stand close to our friends, irrespective of which gender these friends are. Friends will lean towards one another quite naturally in conversation. They will mirror each others' actions and movements. They will look at each other a lot, even if it is only in fleeting glances during conversations with others. The very fact of maintaining a lot of eye contact will, in most cases, be a sign that we are happy with the conversation being conducted. Conversation will flow easily and be relaxed. Men especially will unbutton their jackets or loosen their tie, even going so far as to taking it off when in the company of friends, something they would probably never do in a business situation, and it is often the case that friends will start to dress in a way similar to each other.

In long-standing friendships, there is often less eye contact than with newer friends, unless of course the friends have been parted by distance or external events which means there is a lot to catch up on. There might also be less smiling going on, less touching, but that does not necessarily mean that the friendship is less solid. It is probably a case that the friendship is quite staunch, and that both parties feel greatly at ease with each other. Long-standing friends may sit further apart from each other, voices will be less animated and loud. What is happening is, as with a lot of long-time married couples, we know the other person so well, and they know us, that we no longer adopt the styles customary in newer friendships.

It will be easy for friends to face each other without any feeling of hostility or confrontation. Because friends know each other so well,

this is one of the few times when this sort of positioning will be accepted by another party.

Back to touch

When looking at groups of people, say in a social setting, you may wish to try and work out relationships. Are the people in a romantic involvement? Are they friends?

There are several ways in which you could possibly gauge the answer to these questions. One is obviously to listen in on their conversation. Another way is to look at their positioning, their stance, their general attitude towards each other. Yet another way is to look at how they touch, which does not mean anything if it happens by accident, but how they physically make contact with each other, if indeed they do. Remember that some people just are not touchy types, even if they have a strong friendship or indeed are in a romantic relationship.

When we are friends with someone, we generally will touch each other on the arm or shoulder, although when sitting side by side, a friend may touch us on our leg or knee, especially when a funny incident is being discussed, or in jest. We may also put our arms around their backs, especially if we are guiding them to a table or chair. We may also hug them or link arms when walking along. If we kiss them, we are likely to kiss them on the cheek rather than on the lips. We have moved past the handshake, but not reached the touching of the face, or knee, the more personal parts of the body, and neither have we got to the stage of lip-to-lip kissing or stroking of the body, hair or face. This latter type of touch is normally reserved for those with whom there is a romantic or sexual relationship.

Group friendships

We often have groups of friends who we will socialise with as a group, but not so often as individuals. This is something which may

have happened because the group have a social activity in common, they may be people from our neighbourhood who we meet to walk the dog with, etc. Often groups can tend to become somewhat cliquey – everyone knows everyone else, and to outsiders this can seem to be a hurdle to cross. It is often, for this reason, that newcomers find difficulty in joining an already established group of friends. Commonly in group situations, friends will talk quite animatedly, with lots of loud talk, laughter and smiles. This is especially the case in larger groups. Some groups of people will seem more amenable to newcomers than others. Some would argue that the only way to find this out is to try to become part of the group. However, students of body language will know that by judging the zoning of the group, about which we have already learnt, we will be able to tell whether the group contains friendships of long standing or whether, conversely, the group is made up of people who are together only on a temporary basis, or who are still 'feeling their feet' as a group in their own right. Obviously, it would be more sensible to try to approach a newer group setup, but how do you actually spot the 'new group'. The answer is that newer groups will be made up of people who are standing further apart than the established group. As the people in that group will have less personal knowledge of each other, the voices will be less loud, and there will be less animated lively conversation and laughing.

Whatever the size or development of the group, there will always seem to be someone who is the kingpin of the group at any given time. This could be for various reasons, and it will change dependent upon the situation. Look at a group of people in a bar and decide who is kingpin at any given time. The kingpin of the group will change, given the subject or subjects under discussion.

When joining an existing group, it can often be very difficult for the newcomer. If the newcomer notices what the body language of the group is, how various people sit, stand, behave, talk or whatever, and endeavours to mirror this, the group as a whole will be more likely to accept this person – they will seem to naturally fit in. Should, however, the newcomer show how nervous they are by giving out signals that they feel ill at ease and uncomfortable, this could reflect in their own body language, which would then be

picked up on by the group as a whole, everybody would feel ill at ease with the situation, maybe even defensive or insecure, until the newcomer left. When moving into a group situation as the newcomer, try to watch for the body language signs, be open and smiling as much as possible, and mirror image what is going on within the group. Stand quietly on the fringes of the group, to see whether the group acknowledges your presence. A temporary or friendly group will open up to allow a newcomer to enter, whilst a group of long standing, one sharing secrets or one who feels that newcomers are not acceptable, will not open up. See how conversations ebb and flow between people, what common conversation points are brought up and so on. Common conversation points can be gauged only when the newcomer is within the group, but don't try to force your way into a conversation too soon, which will be seen as threatening to the rest of the group. Asking questions is an easy way to enter into a conversation, and it will also help to get a conversation going.

When given the opportunity to join in any discussion make eye contact with as many of the group as possible, smile as easily and readily as possible, and don't monopolise the conversation for too long, so as not to be seen to be too outspoken or too much of a perceived threat to other members of the group. A good suggestion is to see how previous conversations have started, ended and flowed, and follow suit with your own 'slot'. Remember to watch the other people's expressions, their eye contact and postures. See how close or how far away they are sitting from each other, and watch their movements, gestures and volume and pitch of voice.

Face the people you are talking with, and avoid closed gestures, such as arms folded or legs crossed. Give good eye contact without being seen to be staring, and lean towards the other person when they are speaking, as this will convey interest both in them and what they are saying to you. Try to maintain an interested expression, and watch zoning. Don't cross the zoning barriers too readily and too soon.

If someone you are talking to is looking blankly at you, with no facial expression, little movement and little or no inclusion in the

conversation, they may well be finding you boring. Conversely, other people may well be inclined to fidget, move around a lot, tap their fingers, nod and smile and try to move the conversation on a little to exclude you, but this can also be the case if they have spotted something or someone else they really wish to see and are merely trying to seize the opportunity to talk to that person whilst they are able to. All these things are, however, generally an indication of boredom, as is obviously someone who sits and yawns, although they may just be tired.

A good way of interrupting someone is to keep nodding – one or two nods is quite normal in everyday conversation, but someone who nods three or more times is usually signalling that they want to break into the conversation – watch out for this, and then you will know if you should shut up. Likewise, if you find yourself often being interrupted, especially if you realise that this usually happens when you are talking about one particular subject, you will know then that your conversation is boring, or at least boring to that particular person.

Turning friendships into something more

We will all acknowledge that we react differently with friends away from work than with friends we may have made through work. Although, for most people, we spend a vast part of our daily lives in a work situation, we have a barrier which work colleagues don't often cross, and we seldom tell our work colleagues our secrets. If we tell secrets we have to contend with the possibility of them passing on this information to others within the work place.

In the next chapter, we are going to take a more detailed look at emotions within relationships, and also at how to tell if someone just really needs time to themselves.

PRACTICE

John and Mick are good friends. Mick, however, has another large group of friends he wants John to meet. They arrange to meet everyone at a local bar, but Mick is called away by an urgent business call, just after having introduced John to the group. How should John then proceed to get to know the group, fit in and have a good night out?

Janet and Lesley have been friends for years. They both love dancing and have other similar interests. Lesley has assumed that she will be invited to Janet's house-warming party, and when she hears through another friend that the party is to be an open-house, she feels she should say something to Janet, but does not wish to be confrontational. Disregarding for a moment what the conversation might be, what body language would she be best adopting to avoid any upset? How should she go about it?

5 SIGNALLING EMOTIONS

This chapter will take a more detailed look at the huge range of emotions that we have, how they show themselves up in our body language, and how to spot if there are problems.

In any relationship, whether personal or business, it is useful if you can spot the body language signs of emotional upset and tension. You can then decide whether you feel you should communicate with that other person at that time, or rather wait until what could turn out to be another more suitable time appears. Similarly, it is useful if you can learn to spot the signs that someone just wants to be left alone, and not to approach that person at that time, you can thus save a potentially discordant situation from erupting.

Thinking of emotions

Studies of body language have shown that there are six emotions which cross all boundaries – gender, age, race and nationality. These are sadness, happiness, anger, disgust, fear and surprise. All of us at some time or another will experience these emotions, and they will register in our body language.

All of us have difficulties, at times, distinguishing what emotions are being displayed by the facial expressions alone. We look at other things, such as posture, tenseness or lack of it, what is being said and so on. Men, especially, often don't show their emotions, thinking perhaps that showing grief and upset makes them less masculine or even wimpish. Anger, anxiety and stress, more of

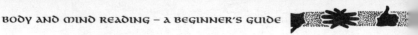

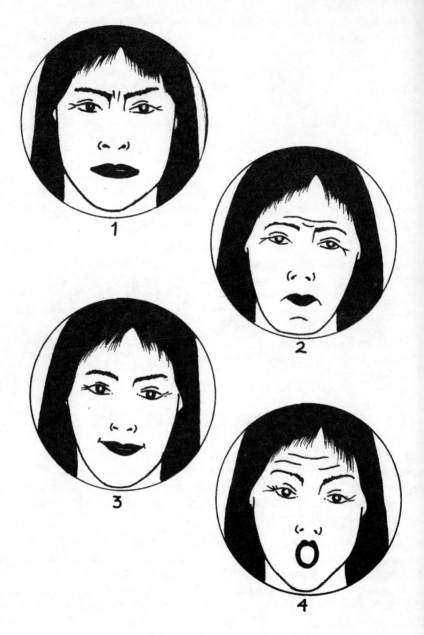

which later, can be shown more easily by men than most other emotions, and it is fair to say that most men will have difficulty in crying openly, if at all.

All emotions affect our bodies. Doctors are well aware that certain emotions, such as prolonged sadness and grief, can affect our bodies and cause difficulties for us. Laughing and being happy will obviously have a beneficial effect, and some doctors now feel that a good laugh can help even those with a long-term illness feel considerably better. Negative emotions, however, will have an opposite effect, especially if repressed or held in, when the body will then be stressed in itself, resulting in various long-term health problems.

Positive emotions, and expressing these openly, are beneficial to us. Scientists acknowledge that when we laugh, we actually take in more oxygen than is normally the case when we merely breathe, and thus we stimulate the circulation, our heart rate increases, and our bodies secrete beneficial hormones. A really good laugh can also cause us to relax, and this is something most of us need, especially in our modern world.

Anger or happiness?

Often our emotions are reflected by our facial expression but errors of judgement can be as high as 40 per cent if facial expressions are judged in isolation. When we are angry, for example, our lips may be tensed together, our whole body will tense, the jaw set, the teeth grit, nostrils flare, and a scowl or frown may show on our face. Our eyes will narrow and inwardly, the stomach may be knotted up, the nerves be at screaming point, so much so that we may end up with a real headache. Look at illustration 1, opposite. If we are angry at someone else, we may gaze at them for some time, and whilst some people would associate red with rage and anger, it is worthwhile remembering that some people can turn quite pale when they are angry. Not only does anger affect us emotionally, but it can cause a rise in blood pressure, arterial changes, respiratory trouble, liver

upsets, changes in the secretion of gall and effects on the pancreas. Anger and rage have been listed by doctors as contributing to, aggravating and even causing such illnesses as asthma, eye afflictions, skin diseases, hives, ulcers and dental and digestive troubles. Rage and fury can upset our logical thoughts so that we cannot form coherent conclusions or pass sound judgement, and often after a period of rage, we suffer a period of extreme mental depression. It is therefore sensible to try to keep our anger, rage and wrath under control. Many times, we can avoid anger outburst by removing ourselves from the situation causing us to feel angry. Doctors are now suggesting that there are various psychological links between anger and cancer, citing those who suffer with cancer as being generally nice people who find difficulty showing their emotions, anger being one of these. Maybe this is something else we should consider when we feel angry.

A good way of dealing with anger when it happens to you is to take out your aggression on something inanimate, and I often wonder if that is why so many people, men especially, work out in the gym after work, where they can lift weights, run on a treadmill or perhaps, depending on the facilities provided, hammer their aggression out on a punchbag. We should, of course, never take our anger out in physical violence towards another person or animal. Whilst voices do raise with anger, and it is often easy to walk away, avoid communication and contact, psychologists suggest that we should always endeavour to talk through our anger, maintain eye contact and deal with the problem objectively.

When we are happy, our eyes are wide open. We smile widely, our eyes crinkle up, we show our teeth with our smile, and we may even laugh. Our whole attitude, our stance, our walk and our behaviour radiates our positive emotion. Happiness is not only reflected in our eyes, our smile and our demenour, but also in our attitude to life and our overall behaviour. Look at illustration 3 on page 64. Those people who are really happy can often be said to have 'a spring in their step' meaning that they seem lighter on their feet and generally more buoyant overall. When we smile, we feel better, and we also make other people feel better – how often do people smile at us to reassure us, for example.

Everyone smiles when happy, even those people who are blind, deaf and unable to speak. There are really three kinds of smiles – the felt smile, the miserable smile and the false smile. It is a fact of life that smiles can be used to try to hide behind, as in the case of someone who smiles through adversity, disappointment or loss, and likewise, there are people who seem able to smile and hold pleasant conversations with those they find difficult or who they dislike. People who work with the public, in the service industries, or perform in public are well used to smiling when they may not, personally, feel the inclination to do so, and consequently we should always bear in mind that a smile may be something to hide our nerves or upset behind.

The felt smile is the real smile – the sort of smile that gives us crinkles around the eyes, opens our mouth a little and shows our teeth.

The simple smile, often seen when people are smiling to themselves over a private thought, is a derivative of the felt smile.

The miserable smile is worn when we are trying to put on a brave face. Whilst we are trying to tell everyone around us that we are fine, in fact we are probably unhappy about something, or even insecure, and seeking to avoid showing our true feelings which would lead to questions we would prefer to do without.

False smiles, part of deceit, last longer than genuine smiles. They are held in place, the lips are stiff and stretched and the eyes will stay unsmiling.

When we meet friends, our smile varies slightly. We can smile showing our top teeth only. The broad smile shows both sets of teeth and the grin is open and wide. This is the sort of smile that often turns into laughter, and someone who smiles like this a lot is likely to be an extrovert. Laughter itself, like smiling, is quite individual, with people often being recognised by their laugh.

Incidentally, studies into smiling and laughter show that women tend to laugh and smile more than men!

When we are happy, our voices also change. We may increase the volume of our voice, speak more quickly, and put more noticeable emphasis on certain words.

Being upset

At some time or another, we will all find ourselves upset. We may cry and we may also, after a bereavement, wish to grieve. This is a natural process, and even before we cry, our eyes will redden, and often seem watery. We also tend to look downwards, generally reducing eye contact, and there is a tendency, especially with children, to want to hug or be hugged. All the upset, grief and unhappiness can come out with crying, and whilst we might be left with red eyes, the resultant benefit for the body is well worthwhile in the long term. When we are sad, our voices will be less loud, we may seem quite slow in speech and our tone will not moderate in pitch. Look at illustration 2 on page 64.

Learning to spot the signs of needing time alone

We all need some time on our own. Some people may claim they are merely recharging their batteries, whilst students of body language will realise that this period of time, called 'downtime' can be either momentary (second to second) or last a longer period of time.

When you need time to yourself on a second-to-second basis, and are in a 'downtime mode', you will possibly tilt your head away from other people, look aside from time to time, shift your shoulders at an angle, but not actively turn away. It should be obvious to other people in your company that perhaps you are merely recalling something from before, remembering things. You are not being hostile, but just need time to yourself for personal reflection perhaps. This is not the same thing at all as dealing with someone who would suggest that they 'know' that people don't like them. What then occurs is that the behaviour of that person is quite marked, and provokes the very reactions from others about which they themselves are so unhappy. By standing or sitting in a position where people cannot talk to you, and by mentally expecting people

to avoid you, they will do so, feeling that you have no time for them at all. Feeling that conversation is likely to prove difficult in any case, these people are awkward when talking to people, will often talk in short sentences, or grunt and become monosyllabic. Because of a lack of self-esteem and feeling that nobody likes them, these people radiate aggression with their behaviour, often coming across as angry, rather than as shy or nervous. Basically, this person has created a self-fulfilling prophecy – an expectation of bad things happening and of being disliked. A similar scenario exists with those who are pessimistic. Optimists create a receptive framework by being outgoing, smiling, hospitable and friendly. They therefore create opportunities for conversation and friendship, as well as creating positive outcomes to situations. Concentrating on the more negative aspects produces a negative behaviour pattern. As Abraham Lincoln said 'Most people are about as happy as they make up their minds to be'.

Someone in a downtime is different, and less aggressive and less hostile. If body language signs of being in a downtime are spotted, the other people would do well to slow down their speech so that the person in the downtime has time to think through their thoughts, and then join back in any conversation that is underway. It will also then be obvious that the people talking have recognised your need to think for a while, and are actively hoping that you will shortly be rejoining the conversation. It should not be assumed that you are feeling tense or stressed, as the signs of being under strain can be more marked.

Showing signs of tension and stress

When we are under strain, as with periods of downtime, we do tend to angle our bodies away from other people. However, when in a period of strain in a working situation especially, we will actively turn our back on other people, in order to be able to get on with the

task in hand without intrusion or interruption. Often our head may seem hazy – we will not be able to think clearly. We will also avoid eye contact with other people, as by avoiding eye contact with others, there is less likelihood of them trying to engage us in conversation, which would put further pressure on us. We need to be able to concentrate on the things in hand. We may well also shut down in our hearing. We just won't hear what other people are saying, and we may also be too busy to notice that other people are even in the room, or occasionally, during periods of excessive strain, we won't notice someone touching us on the arm or shoulder.

It is important that, when we feel under pressure in a working situation, other people realise that if we don't get this seclusion from others, we are likely to become nervous, tense and even irritated. You only have to approach someone when they are working to a deadline, for instance, to find them snap at you and show their annoyance at your interruption.

Physical barriers may also be created, such as crossed legs, elbows sticking out at a severe angle to increase the personal space occupied. Along with a look of intense concentration, there may also be frowns, and shoulders may well be raised.

Most often it is useful if the person who is under strain explains the situation to others before a problem arises. It you tell people you are going to be busy, they are less likely to think that you are being off-hand with them and take your snapping answers personally. It is often best to just steer clear of people when they are showing such obvious signs of being under strain.

It is important when you see that someone is obviously under strain, but need to have a brief conversation with them over something, that you watch your zoning areas. Even if you are really close to that other person, it would be well advised for you to stay within the social zoning area rather than entering a closer zone. Any conversation would be well advised to be short, and you should then see how it goes from there and what sort of response you get. Keep well back from that person, and don't crowd them, which could add to their feeling of tension and strain.

Stress, however, especially long-term stress, is another thing. Stress is often called 'the silent killer' because of its ability to cause dramatic physical symptoms and illnesses, such as heart attacks, gastro-intestinal problems, insomnia, migraine, ulcers, asthma, arthritis, depression, and allergies. One's emotional state can, doctors assure us, play a large part in skin disorders, and many doctors now believe that stress is often a factor in a number of skin conditions, including hives, psoriasis, acne and eczema. Stress also suppresses the immune system, leaving us more open to infections, colds and 'flu. In this modern age, we are all subject to certain stresses. For some people going to work is stressful, whilst for others, the prospect of not having work creates the stress.

When we are under severe stress, our whole attitude and character can change. Acute stress often results from the strains of everyday life, and often involves unpleasant situations that need to be resolved, but at the time, are not so easy to solve. We become short tempered on a more permanent basis, we suffer from tension in the shoulders, we are hostile towards people, will not socialise as much,

if at all, and those under stress may often be seen with their head in their hands, running their hands through their hair and gritting their teeth. When under stress, we often have tight lips, tense shoulders. We seem heavy in our movement, and our voice may rise in both pitch and volume. We may also slam around and become generally very noisy. Colleagues and partners who spot these signs of tension in those around them would do well to remember to consider open doors as closed, even if this is not the case. Wait for the person concerned to speak to you first, rather than making the first approach.

Whilst too much stress can be harmful, we do need some stress in our lives to be able to function effectively, but on a short-term basis. It is part of our physical makeup, and part of what psychologists call the 'flight or fight syndrome'. Stress and its effect on our lives are something that many people study in isolation, and the advent of stress counselling shows that we often don't know how to successfully deal with stresses and strains we meet on a daily basis. We all experience stress in limited amounts when we are fearful over something which has happened (rather than being fearful over something which has yet to happen which is more concern and anxiety than fear), when we are shocked or surprised. See illustration 4, page 64.

Chronic stress can be long term, with the sufferer seeing no way out of a stressful situation, whether it relates to job, lack of employment or problematic personal relationships.

Current UN statistics suggest that stress has become one of the most serious health issues of the twentieth century, with an estimated $200 billion dollars being lost in the US alone due to stress-related illnesses. A French survey revealed that 64 per cent of nurses and 61 per cent of teachers find their work environment stressful, and suggested that women across the globe suffer more from stress than men, probably because of their need to juggle home and work lives.

All this can lead to depression, the signs of which are lethargy, a tendency to either shout or cry easily, a feeling of worthlessness and many other such signs – all of which are obvious from the posture of the sufferer, their reaction to situations and the way in which they respond in conversation.

Within the last few years, we have also learned more about PTSD – post traumatic stress disorder – with many people who have witnessed a traumatic event or who have learnt about it through photographs, as well as those who have been actually involved in an accident or disaster. Many soldiers and those in the armed services now speak of suffering from PTSD, as do those who have been assaulted, raped or subjected to child abuse, and these people can continue to suffer severe problems many years after the event which sparked off the initial problem.

Doctors suggest that stress can be helped, and in most cases beaten, if a healthy diet is adopted, exercise is taken on a regular basis and sufficient sleep is obtained. It is also important, especially if the stress revolves around work issues, to get organised, as people who manage their time are much better able to cope with stress. We also need support, and during stressful times, those who have a close social network gain at least a measure of protection against becoming overwhelmed.

In order to combat stress on a permanent basis, we often need to be more balanced, more reasonable, realising our limitations and placing no extra demands on ourselves than we feel we are reasonably able to handle. We should also learn not to compare ourselves with others, as we all have our own gifts and abilities, and trying to keep up with someone else, whether it is materialistically, competitively or within a working situation can cause problems. Often, a complete change in our thinking is required, and we may have to learn new ways of reacting to circumstances, so that they do not continue to overwhelm us. We especially need to make time for relaxation, and I would suggest those people with stress-related problems consider reading *Spiritual Healing*, *Visualisation*, *Meditation* and *The Healing Power of Plants*, other books within this series.

When under stress at work, a good idea is to send your calls to the answerphone, if you are able. If you are in an office environment, and are lucky to have your own office, close the door, and maybe even lie down. Those people who are not so lucky may wish to make an escape to the cloakroom, where the action of running cold water across the wrist area may also help.

At times of severe stress, try to think about nice things – recall happy times and practise visualisation techniques. Stretch, breathe deeply and regularly, and try relaxation exercises. People who have their hands tightly clenched, as in the case of stress sufferers, are very difficult to relate to, and consequently can become isolated within the community. Remember that when people are under stress, especially severe stress, the last thing they want from other people is to be questioned as to whether they are all right or not. It just adds to the pressure. Wait until the person concerned starts off any conversation, and even then, words should be chosen carefully. All this requires patience and we must wait until the other person wants to talk.

Nervousness, tension, depression, fear and anxiety

We all get nervous at some time or other in our lives. Nervous gestures can include rapid movements, crossing of arms and legs, looking away from other people, moving around and fidgeting when seated, moving toward the edge of a seat rather than relaxing into it, playing with objects, nervous smoking, and pointing of body towards the nearest exit.

Public speakers will be well aware of nervous signs – clearing the throat, constantly taking small sips of water, quick glances around the room, rubbing of the nose to indicate doubt, and jangling money in pockets are just some of these. All these things are quite normal and can be easily spotted. Nervous speakers will also tend to 'um' and 'er' more than more seasoned speakers, and often at the end of their talk sigh quite audibly, glad that the ordeal is over.

We have already briefly covered aspects of depressive behaviour, but it is worthwhile pointing out that those people who are suffering from depression need reassurance and upbeat conversation from

those around them. It should be remembered that someone who is constantly fed negative and depressing thoughts, someone who is told they look ill or tired, is likely to become ill and/or tired, if they weren't so already. Any improvement in their condition is likely to be negated by such comments. People who are depressed are likely to be slow in their movement, often looking downwards when moving. Their posture will be slumped, their eyes hazy or watery. They will find difficulty in smiling, they will be apathetic to any suggestions and will either, depending on their character, be very talkative about their problems or conversely sink into a world of their own with no conversation being possible. The mouth will be turned down at the corners, and in cases of extreme depression and sadness, there will be tears, trembling of the lips and a wish to hide the face. Those trying to help such people would be well advised not to use phrases like 'I understand what you are going through'. Everybody's reactions are different, and even fellow sufferers of depression cannot understand what another individual is feeling. Similarly comments suggesting you should 'pull yourself together' should be avoided. A good way of combating negative thoughts, if you are able, is when you realise you are thinking negatively, say 'stop', even speaking aloud if you feel this would help. Some people imagine that they see a neon sign, flashing 'stop' in front of their eyes. Psychiatrists and students of psychology suggest that because the word 'stop' carries such prohibitive thoughts, it serves to stop us in our tracks from the direction of our thinking.

Fear is something we can all relate to, even if it's only a feeling we encounter when watching late-night horror films! When we are frightened, our eyes tend to open widely, stare perhaps, as if we need to take in more of the scene before us. We may also tense up, jump back, or even run away. Again, look at illustration 4 on page 64. Men may, when in a frightening situation, merely tense up, ready for a fight, whilst those of us who are less assertive will most definitely run away! It is, however, fair to say that fear shows up in different ways with different people. Anxiety, a form of fear, is a little more subtle, giving us feelings of tenseness in the stomach, nervous indigestion, and other such annoying symptoms. All these emotions, and more, show on our faces. Fear can be quite a good thing, and it

is worthwhile remembering that fear can cause someone to proceed with more caution in the face of danger, and thereby avoid a potential pitfall. Likewise, fear can also be morbid, destroying hope and weakening the nervous sytem.

Fear is something which we can bring upon ourselves, and if we seek to remember bad experiences, when faced with the same situation again, fear can overwhelm us, and the result may be something even worse than was previously the case.

Many people, for example, have a terrible fear of flying. Some others have a fear of water, fearing that they will drown. Such fears can make us physically sick with worry, so much so that at the sight of an airport, some people with a fear of flying can be actually sick with fear. They will tremble, their breathing rate will increase, they may turn pale in complexion, and their eyes will dart about, seeking to find a way out of the situation. In their imagination, they are already on the plane, it will no doubt crash, and they will be killed. Such ingrained fears often need professional medical assistance in order for relief to be gained.

Fear should not necessarily be confused with anxiety. You can generally spot fear from looking into the eyes of someone, as is also the case with unhappiness and sadness. Fear can also include alarm, dread and disquiet.

Anxiety is often associated with a fear that something unknown is going to happen, and thus is often based on probabilities rather than on past events. Most times, people don't know what they are anxious about. They will spend time worrying over things likely to happen, or conversely about things which did happen which they cannot change. Anxiety attacks then turn into acute nervousness – trembles, clammy hands, headaches and even physical sickness. Many people who have worries about their health become overly anxious when any new symptom appears – it must be something dreadful, even if it is only the signs of a mild cold. Exam nerves are another form of anxiety – the mind going blank and tensing up, causing an increased heart rate, sweating and bad performance. Other nerve-racking things can include getting married, cooking an important meal, making a speech.

Whilst anxiety includes fear, this fear is often vague, making us uneasy. Adrenalin is produced by our bodies, the muscles tense, often causing trembling, and sometimes a feeling of achiness. The heart will beat faster, our breathing will speed up, our digestive system will seem to go into overdrive, and we may then get cramps, diarrhoea and nausea, as well as feeling dry in our mouth. We may also have a knitted brow, and general unhappy look, although it is worthwhile considering that a knitted brow may also be a sign of a headache or general feeling of being unwell. Panic attacks can often result from anxiety, yet if you go along with the feeling, refusing to give in, the symptoms will pass quite quickly, and you will return to normal. If, however, you become more fearful, you will worsen your condition, and suffer longer periods of anxiety. Similarly, long periods of anxiety can lead to depression, which will rob a person of their strength and motivation. Anxiety can raise or lower blood pressure, can elevate the white blood cell count, can affect the blood sugar by the action of adrenalin on the liver, and can even change an electro-cardiogram. Anxiety, being a form of worry, affects the circulation, the heart, the glands and the whole nervous system.

A little anxiety is, however, quite natural, and we will all feel anxious over certain things, especially when we are concerned about other people. Concern can often be beneficial, in that it leads us to loving acts of hospitality, a generous spirit and willingness to help others. Likewise, it is also quite normal to find oneself anxious over providing for the family the necessities of life – food, clothing, shelter and so on, but it is not advisable to become too bogged down with such things, and we would all do well to remember the difference between what are really necessities and what are, in fact, merely wants.

It is often worthwhile remembering that if we are fearful and anxious, especially if we are thinking of success in an undertaking, or attaining something we really want to attain, then subconsciously, the thought that we will fail will be registered. Again, creative visualisation and relaxation programmes can help with states of fear and anxiety, and remember, many of the things we worry about never happen. You cannot change the past, and the future is yet to come. All you can do something about is the present. Stop thinking

about 'what if' and concentrate on 'what is'. It is good advice to think of every day as potentially your last, and don't waste it. Keeping busy is one of the best antidotes I know to helping with negativity, fear, anxiety and depression.

Spotting anxiety, fear and depression in other people can cause those people with warm hearts to want to help more than perhaps is healthy. Whilst it is an admirable quality in anybody to want to help another, and many people indeed get a great deal of satisfaction from sharing the worries and troubles of other people, it is quite another thing to allow yourself to become personally distressed and distraught over problems which are not your own. We cannot do everything for other people, and it is a pointless and fruitless exercise worrying about things which are out of our control. Taking on other people's depression and unhappiness can make our own lives very unhappy. It is also important to point out that some people can deliberately set out to manipulate others by presenting their problems as if they belonged to the other party, thus making that other person guilty, anxious or even unhappy as a result.

When we are nervous, tense, anxious or fearful, crossing our arms, legs and ankles locked, hiding behind a newspaper, fidgetting, jangling coins and so on become the norm. Spotting such signs in someone, we should endeavour to be brief in our contact, reassuring and warm, offering a smile readily and also, depending upon the person, a touch of support.

Deceit

Spotting the signs of deceit can be quite difficult, as some people, unfortunately, are more accomplished in the art of being deceitful than others, leading to many mistakes being made.

It is fair to say that the face is almost always the area where emotions will register, especially where deceit is concerned. Clearly identify the signs, and don't assume that because someone is looking away all the time and seems nervous and/or preoccupied that they are being deceitful.

It is generally accepted that, at some point in time, most people are deceitful. Children may well persistently try to deceive their parents, and it is normally the case that a parent will be able to spot immediately if their child is 'trying to pull the wool over their eyes' by their facial expression, their speech pattern, their hand movements and their inability to look at their parent.

It is suggested that, when people are attempting to deceive, they may talk less and smile more than would normally be the case, and they may also stumble over their words a little more than normal.

Someone who is being deceitful will find it difficult to maintain eye contact. They will not look at us when we are talking, nor when they are talking, and may often be looking downwards. It is also worthwhile considering the smile – the false or insincere smile when talking about cases of deceit. Smiles can often be used to mask other emotions, and many people, especially those who work within the public sector and with the public generally, may have received special training enabling them to more easily smile in cases of stress.

In the case of someone trying to be open, there may often be an open-handed signal – this shows honesty. When people are being honest, their hands will be on show. Those who are, by the other token, being dishonest or deceitful, may feel guilty and thus try to hide their hands by either putting their hands behind their backs, in their pockets, or having their arms folded. However, it is worthwhile considering that someone who is trying to deceive may seek to do so by actually showing his hands, palms upwards, and shrugging, as if to say that they can't help themselves, and enlist our sympathy for their case.

Someone being underhanded may also wish to cover their mouths in speech, and the hand that normally coves the mouth is the left hand, irrespective of whether the person concerned is right or left handed.

Similarly, someone who is being deceitful and lying will possibly move their feet, torso and legs around a lot. This is a sign of feeling uncomfortable, and pointing a toe or limb towards the nearest exit will underline the fact that the person concerned wishes to get the conversation over with and leave. They may well rub the side of their

nose, their eyes, hold the back of their neck, or clutch their throat, lick their lips or even sweat profusely, all because they feel uncomfortable with their deceit. As such, they will try to keep a distance between themselves and their audience, so as to maintain a barrier of safety.

I cannot emphasise enough how vital it is to make sure that you take into account all the signs being displayed, as, for example, the open-handed gesture with shoulder shrug on its own is not a sign of deceitfulness, but more a case of being unable to say anything about a situation. Similarly, the person who blushes, perspires, sweats, trembles and stutters may well just be nervous, and not bent on deceiving his or her audience. To spot a liar or deceiver, listen to what they say, how they say it, whether their speech pattern is different from what is normal for them, whether they are maintaining a distance which again would be abnormal for them, and look for closed and negative gestures.

PRACTICE

During the course of this chapter, we have looked at several emotions. Before we move on to look at working relationships, let's take a few case studies to complete our chapter.

John comes into the office after a day's absence. He had telephoned in to work the previous day saying that he felt ill with a migraine. Brian, his boss, thinks that he merely took the day off because he wanted to see a friend who had been in the area the previous day on a short holiday. Brian calls John in to his office to ask him whether he is feeling any better, and asks whether there is anything that the others in the office can do to help John if he is still not feeling well. What signs should Brian look for to see if John was being truthful over his illness and absence from work?

For some time, Gloria has been rather uncommunicative with Steve. They always had a fairly good relationship until recently, and all of a sudden, Steve notices that Gloria doesn't respond in the same way to touch, gestures of affection and suggestions that they spend time together and talk. Why should Steve not jump to the conclusion that Gloria is having an affair, if these are the only signs he has spotted? What other signs should he look for if he felt that Gloria were being unfaithful, and what are the potential dangers? What could be some of the reasons for Gloria's change in behaviour?

6 BODY LANGUAGE AND WORK

During the course of this chapter, we will be taking a look at various aspects of working life, and seeing how something as obvious as the seating arrangement at work can have an affect on how we are seen by others, and how they respond to us. We will also consider the caring professions, and take a look at the boss.

REACTING WITH OTHERS — LOOKING AT THE NEW EMPLOYEE AND WORKMATES

When we are at work, we all meet other people. For many of us, those people are the people we work with every day, but for others, especially those in the caring professions, they may never see the other people again, or only rarely. How we react to them will affect their opinions of us as people and also as professionals within our industry, whatever that industry is, and it is therefore important for all of us to try to learn about each other, learn how to give reassurance, how to listen and how to react to others, if we are to have a successful and stress-free working life. We all need to learn the non-verbal communication skills which will make us successful in our interactions with others, so that we may be in a better position to discern whether people are hiding things, whether they

are being truthful, whether they are creating barriers and how to get the best out of other people.

Many companies have strict dress codes, and for this reason many will provide uniforms, so that some element of conformity is produced. Remember that style creates a statement, not only about you, but in a work place situation, it also creates a statement about the business.

If there is a certain freeness with dress codes, especially if starting a new job, take the lead from the people already there and dress accordingly. Watch colours, lengths and styles. Not only then will you fit in with them and they will feel you are a part of an established team, but you will also fit in with the company's image.

When it comes to people in authority within a company, some bosses will have their own offices or suites of offices, removed from the hub of the rest of the business. Often these offices or suites of offices will be on a higher floor, as if there is an invisible ladder which people have climbed up. This is generally seen as the company where prestige matters, where those who are on a higher rung within the corporate ladder wish to make it plain that they have 'made it' or at least are heading that way. Things such as names on doors, name plates on desks will be visible, and it is important, no matter what the business situation or company, to make sure that a new employee especially sees what the pecking order is between the different members of staff and observes the barriers created. Look at who gets on with whom and try to match and mirror them. Remember to observe all the time and as with joining any new group, don't rush to join in conversations, especially not voicing your own opinion too soon. It is always a good idea not to try to infiltrate large groups until a reasonable period has elapsed. Look at smaller groups where there is less hierarchy, and if you can, try to get to talk to people on a one-to-one basis before joining in with any group situation. Remember, when you are dealing with only one other person, or are in a small group, studying body language will be a lot easier than if you were with a large group of people.

Try to be friendly. Initially, you may not know the pecking order of the company, and awful situations can arise by being too friendly too soon. Those people in higher positions may listen to you but interrupt when you speak. Those in lower positions will pay attention and not interrupt, and you will always know when you are respected, because the other person will nod and smile and immediately take up any suggestion you make as being valid for consideration, if not in fact action. Even amongst staff of similar capabilities, there will be a pecking order, and by observation this should become apparent. People higher up in the pecking order will breeze into an office without an appointment, will not feel the need to knock on the boss' door so readily. A little time observing what is going on will soon identify matters. Be aware of office politics and don't force yourself into a situation which would create tension for either yourself or others. The best advice is to try to be friendly to everybody, don't get involved in office politics and remember that we work to live, not live to work. If, however, you are joining a workforce where team work is important, do try to fit in with their dress code and appearance, as not only will you be more readily accepted, but interaction will flow more smoothly, as you will not be seen to be an outsider so much.

When someone new joins an existing team of employees, there are often many stresses of which the newcomer is unaware which could affect his or her feelings about the new job. For example, they may have taken a job which internal applicants had applied for and been rejected for, and as a result, those people who were not considered suitable for the post may well feel quite hostile towards the new employee. Although it is not his or her fault, this hostility can be quite marked, and the newcomer may well wonder why people are not being very friendly. Rivalries will occur all too frequently if you are not careful, especially if people feel threatened by 'the new kid on the block'. As a result, new employees should be careful to watch for those quick smiles of congratulations which really have jealous undertones. By the same token, the new employee may have replaced someone who has been with the company years and who was well liked, well respected and competent, and as the new employee, you cannot possibly begin to fill that space immediately.

All you can do is try to make sure that you face people directly when they are talking to you, maintain as much eye contact as possible, lean towards them when they speak, smile and seem confident. It is also worthwhile remembering that the working environment you have inherited pre-dates you. You can, however, if the situation permits, change small things about your seating position for example, add a plant or two to your area, but remember not to encroach on other people's areas, and also that whilst you may wish to imprint your own personality on your working space, it is not fair to try to imprint that personality throughout the whole of an office, if for example, you only take up a corner of that office.

Dealing with the boss

Not all bosses will have name plates on the door, but those who do may well also have a big desk, appear autocratic, critical and unapproachable. This is not a general scenario, but you may well encounter these people, especially in a business setting. These are the less liberal bosses. Knock on the door before you enter. Wait until you are asked to sit down before doing so, and wait before you speak. Should you find your boss on the telephone when you enter, and notice that your boss is opening and closing the top drawer, it is a sure sign that there is a problem somewhere, and you would be well advised to be careful with your conversation. Even when he or she finally shuts the desk draw and commences a conversation with you, it is fair to say that the problem will still be on his or her mind. Remember to maintain your distance, and look again at what we have learnt about zoning in an earlier chapter. Remember to be businesslike and clear.

Also remember that it will be important to be punctual. Nobody respects those who are always late, as it reflects on your own efficiency and ability to cope with the work you are employed to undertake. Similarly, those people who always come into work early and leave late may be either trying to 'get in with the boss' or unable to fulfil all their duties within the allotted time, and thus be

considered inefficient, especially if they always seem to be behind with their workload, irrespective of the hours they put in.

Democratic bosses are more social types. They may well have plants in their office, pictures of their families on the desk, and by that I don't mean formal photographs, but more the average holiday snapshot picture. These are the bosses that will tell you things, rather than send you memos. They will come out of their office and approach you, rather than asking for you to come to them. They will also laugh with other members of staff, even touch others and offer congratulations when a job is well done. Helping to create a happy atmosphere, telling people they have done a good job can be really motivating, and say a lot more than one might think. It shows that the boss is genuinely happy with you and values your work and contributions, especially if a friendly pat on the shoulder is included. Democratic bosses, those who want their workforce to work well, are likely to be open in their gestures, supportive in voice and behaviour and have a more positive and friendly facial expression. They will feel in control, be able to move about in their chair as they speak, confident of their position and their authority. It has been noticed in studies that those who feel dominant or confident of themselves, especially when in the presence of other people, will have their feet on the desk when they speak, and this will also include periods when they are using the telephone.

Democratic bosses also endeavour to be motivational in approach, engendering a feeling in their workforce of wanting to do something and do it well, rather than giving out the message that this is something they have to do as part of their contract. Remember, however, that this person is still the boss, and be careful. Be friendly, by all means, but also be aware that they are in a higher position than you and are worthy of your respect. Be self-sufficient and motivated, and always appear confident about what you are doing in your work and how you conduct yourself. Confidence is an important asset. Many times, it is worthwhile considering that those people who seem supremely confident are, in essence, as scared as we are, but are more capable of bluffing a situation than others. Practise being confident, and go back to what we said in an earlier chapter about going into places on your own and meeting strangers.

To appear confident, all you have to remember is to stand firm and square. Try to look sharp and awake and breathe deeply, especially if you are to enter a situation of tension, such as a meeting or interview. Although your mouth may be dry, try to speak slowly and smile. As with public speaking, if in a meeting situation, wait until after you have finished speaking before taking any drinks of water.

Dealing with the public

Those people who work with the public on a daily basis such as social workers, nurses, doctors, counsellors, advisors, bus-drivers, shop assistants and so on will come into contact with a wider band of people than someone who goes to work in an office or factory environment. These people will, because of their job and also maybe because of training, have acquired the skill of being able to maintain eye contact with strangers, smile, be open and confident, assertive and firm yet understanding, and will also possibly have gained a lot of knowledge of body language during the course of their working lives. People in sales especially may have attended courses and seminars on how to make the client feel at ease, how to close a sale, how to meet clients' needs. They will know how to be all things to all people, how to act with one set of circumstances in a different way to how they would act with another group or individual given the same set of circumstances. They will know all about seating arrangements to create the best advantage and they will also know how to reassure people. Similarly, those who deal with the public by telephone, such as receptionists and telesales people will know how to talk to people, when to listen and when to interrupt and what questions to ask in order to know the best course of action. Obviously, their body language will not be seen, but they will not slump in their chairs and doodle whilst talking, because this will come across in the voice as being disinterested. Studies show that most people who doodle when using the telephone do so because they are bored, frustrated or plain disinterested. They will remain alert and focused on their caller, and may well even gesture with their hands naturally as they speak. Their appearance, especially if they are receptionists, will be quite important. This covers not only

their clothing and style, but also their physical appearance. They need to look cheerful and happy in their jobs.

Knowing how to nod in agreement, listening to how the conversation flows and coming in at the point in the conversation where the speech is slowing down is all something people who work with the public need to know instinctively how to do. Nurses and counsellors will know when to offer a hand of support – they will be able to read situations and people effectively. Their heads may well be tilted during conversations showing their interest and concern, and they will place themselves in a seating position where closeness can be observed although not encroaching on personal zoning areas.

One of the most important aspects of body language if you are in a profession where you meet people all the time is eye contact. It is vital that you maintain eye contact as much as possible. If you are offering reassurance, you should smile. Similarly, if you are selling a product or a service, you should consider how people will view you. You should remember that your appearance, dress and grooming will have an effect on how people view you as a professional within your field. Whilst many social workers tend to dress in a way so as not to create hostility and barriers with their clients, they would not, for example, wear ripped jeans, even if they were all the trend at the time. Dressing casually does not mean being sloppy. An over-casual appearance will lead to people forming an opinion that you are not good in your job. Whilst you may have to deal with someone's problems – this could be their personal problems if you are in a counsellor's job or their dissatisfaction with a product or service if you are in a sales-related job, it is important to remember that every one of your customers deserves your personal attention, and you should never rush through one client or customer because you want to get on with the next thing, or by the same token, feel the need to be less attentive because you have placed yourself in a position of being late for another appointment. Your stress will show to that customer or client, and the end result may be affected.

Those dealing with the public also need to be tactful. Tact is really discerning what is appropriate to say or do in dealing with other people. It also means being able to deal with others without giving offense. We should be careful never to cause hurt feelings or cause

offense by the manner in which we say or do things. Those people who deal with the public on a day-to-day basis at work should not allow their personal problems to infringe on their working performance and the way in which they deal with their clients or customers. Someone who remains calm under trying circumstances is most likely to win another person over to his point of view, and especially in a sales job, this is important. Being hotheaded or excitable will possibly lead to antagonism. Should it be a situation where the customer is angry, it is necessary to be tactful yet firm, and whilst compromise may be necessary, the initial approach is to try to understand why that person is feeling as they are, and perhaps even ask questions to ascertain the full extent of the problem. Someone who is tactful will also encourage feedback and conversation, and those who work with the public may well have cultivated the art of thinking from the viewpoint of those to whom they are speaking, thus being better able to understand and form a good communicative structure.

We should also remember that the right word spoken at the right time can have quite dramatic results, and therefore our choice of words needs to accurately express our thoughts. This is not always easy, takes effort, and good judgement on occasions, but one good rule is to keep words simple. They need not be complicated or difficult in order to get the point across.

Seating arrangements

Where seats are arranged can be vital in achieving a good result, especially in meeting situations, in counselling sessions and in encouraging teamwork. People tend to place themselves in a position which is advantageous to them. For example in meetings or situations where they are likely to feel uncomfortable, they will place themselves in a corner, at the back of a room or out of general vision.

Round tables mean that everybody can see everyone else. There are no corners, no blind spots. There is no competition between people. There is no feeling of threat, and consequently, therefore, no need for people to feel defensive. This is the best seating arrangement for

persuasive discussions to take place. However, with square and oblong tables, this is not always the case, and some seating positions can create tension and friction. Whilst everyone can interact around a square table, an atmosphere of competition or defensiveness can be created, and so this is the seating arrangement best used if it is intended that conversations be kept short.

Let's look at a square-shaped table. The person who wishes to talk to everyone will position himself as shown on illustration 1 opposite, at position A. The person who wishes to co-operate with that person will sit alongside at position B. The person sitting at C in a slight corner position can also control the group, but has the disadvantage of not having a co-operator by her side. The person sitting in position D can be seen as being in direct competition to A. This is quite a defensive position. E, on the other hand, is in an independent position. This is the seat chosen by the person who doesn't want to interact with the others, wants to be alone, has no interest or possibly has hostility towards the others at the table. It is interesting to note how many people, entering a library to read, will choose this seating position if they find another person sitting at the only table available for use.

It is also fair to say that the person sitting at position C can engage in friendly casual conversation with everyone. She has unlimited eye contact, it will be easy for gestures (nobody is sitting next to her who may be hindered by arm movements). She has also, however, created a barrier because she is sitting on her own.

Those people who work together a lot, work well together and are used to each other's ways of working will choose to adopt the A B seating plan. This is a good seating position if you are sure that there is no need to keep your eye on the other person, and no element of competition is involved. On the other hand, salesmen who wish to give a good presentation to a prospective client will tend to create a corner seating plan, as shown opposite.

If in a situation where it is necessary to have back-up from others, the sales person will sit either at position B1 or B2 as shown on illustration 3 opposite, leaving room for the back-up person to sit at position C, with the client immediately opposite them in position A. By sitting thus, the sales person can co-operate with everyone.

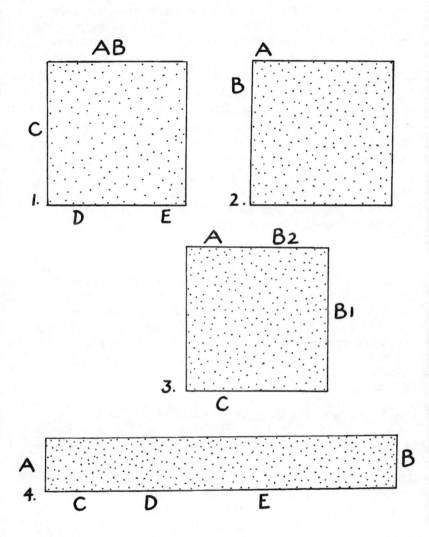

Should the table be rectangular, as in illustration 4 on page 91, and five people, for example, be there for a productive discussion, the following suggestion would work well. A or B could be the person in charge. Moving down in authority would be C or E if sitting next to B.

If wishing to get the best from a one-to-one meeting, sitting immediately across a table can be seen as defensive or competitive, and show that a firm stance is being taken. It is not a seating position which encourages informality, but more a seating arrangement likely to create resistance or hostility from the person opposite. This is the sort of seating position one sees in offices, where the boss calls in the employee and places him or her directly opposite, giving the protection of the desk and status for the boss, and putting the employee in a position where eye contact or lack of it will be immediately spotted. As a result, the employee may immediately feel that he or she has done something wrong and is to be reprimanded.

Should a barrier in the middle of the desk be created in any way, dividing the territories of the desk, and this can be anything from a lot of paperwork or a plant to a series of photographs, with nothing being allowed to cross that barrier, co-operation and agreement is not likely, and is not planned. In order to break down the dividing line, it is necessary to put things across the barrier, although in some situations this can create a threat, as in the case of allowing someone to hurl a letter terminating their employment back at the person who has given it.

It is also worthwhile noting that a person's blood pressure can increase if they are seated with their back to an open space. Seated in that position, they are not able to see who is coming up from the rear, and cannot see what else is happening within the room. As a result, should someone be positioned there intentionally in a business meeting, it is fair to assume that the person who has suggested that seating plan is trying to undermine that person. This is particularly evident if they are seated with their back to an open door or with their back to a window at ground-floor level. All sorts of things may be happening behind their back, and they could well be taken advantage of.

In counselling situations or where there is the need for reassurance, having chairs positioned away from a table is a good idea. Taking illustration 2 on page 91 and removing the table, one would have an angled seating position, there would be no element of competition or need for defensiveness, yet the seating may be close enough to allow some contact but not too close to feel threatening. This is also the best way to make sure that everything is clearly understood if there is a need to emphasise a point, as you can see that person's body in full, can fully judge by their body language what affect your conversation is having on them, and not be limited to mere facial expressions.

Getting a job — attending interviews

So far we have concentrated our look at the work place from the standpoint of someone already in employment. However, this is not always the case, and for the majority of us, at some time or another we will be faced with the interview situation. We may want to project ourselves as we really are, but also present the best image to suit the company.

When we apply for a job, we normally have a good idea of who or what the company are. Judgements made from the advert alone are often good enough starting points, and if we are lucky enough to actually be near enough to see what the building is like and what the outside appearance suggests, we will also be able to build on our mental picture of what the firm is saying, what they represent, and what they expect of their employees. Similarly, if we know other people who work there, we can learn a great deal about a place.

Confidence in interview is really important. Making sure that you are calm and composed is essential, and so is presentation, both of yourself and of any documents you might be leaving for assessment. Try to make sure that you sit tall, don't slump or slouch, and neither should you sit forward in your chair, as you could be considered too

anxious. If the employer has tried to create an environment of relaxation where the interviewee is not too stressed, he or she may well have an angled seating arrangement, but by using this strategy, the interviewee, if nervous, will be more open to observation. Try not to move around and remember to smile. Keep eye contact with the interviewer, listen to what they are saying, and make sure you answer clearly. Studies suggest that people tend to remember the last thing said, so when you are about to leave, make sure that your parting comments make the right impression, and remember to shake hands. Try to smile at the receptionist when you enter and when you leave, and if there is insufficient seating for you to sit down and wait for your interview, at least make sure that you move well into the room, as standing by the door could make it appear that you are uncomfortable and wish to leave at the earliest opportunity. Make sure also that you are polite and friendly with any other staff members who might be introduced to you or who you may meet on arrival.

When dealing with people as part of your job you may wish to look at the following list of do's and dont's:

HINDERING BEHAVIOUR

- Lean away with hands clenched, arms and legs crossed
- Look at the other person for less than 50 per cent of the time
- Listen silently
- Interrupt
- Have a blank expression
- Sit opposite the other person
- Don't use the other person's name
- Use the other person's name artificially
- Don't ask questions
- Ask closed questions
- Don't check understanding
- Stick rigidly to saying things that are routine and standard
- Don't acknowledge the other person's expressed feelings or point of view

- Acquiesce
- Never explicitly agree with the other person
- Pick holes in the other person's ideas
- Criticise the other person
- Disagree first, then say why
- Be defensive and never admit to any inadequacy
- Be secretive and withhold information
- Remain aloof
- Don't give the other person anything

helpinG behaviouR

- Lean forward with hands open, arms and legs uncrossed
- Look at the person for approximately 60 per cent of the time
- Smile
- Sit beside the person or at a 90° angle to him or her
- Use the other person's name early on
- Ask open questions
- Summarise
- Refer back to what the other person has said
- Show empathy
- When in agreement, openly say so and why
- Build on the other person's ideas
- Be non-judgemental
- If you disagree, give the reason first then say that you disagree
- Admit when you don't know the answer or have made a mistake
- Openly explain what you are doing or intend to do
- Give the other person something – name card or notes

GLOBAL OVERVIEW

We are nearing the end of our journey of discovering the basics of body language, but there is still a lot to learn, and I really must stress that further reading on the subject is recommended. However, before we end our discussions, we should take a look at other countries as, in this ever shrinking world, we will inevitably come across people from other cultures and other lands, and should take a brief look at differences.

In various parts of the world, we are often in danger of saying something which makes us look silly, and whilst it is admirable to learn to speak as many languages as fluently as possible so that business and personal relationships run smoothly, there can still be problems. For example, tutting in Syria (making a *tsk* sound) is actually an everyday term for no, and so someone making that noise to a Syrian would not be showing disgust or repugnance, but actually just saying no. Similarly, it is unfortunate that body language within differing cultures can also cause us problems. For example, shaking the head to most people indicates 'no', but in Greece, Turkey and Bulgaria, this does not apply and to signal 'no', the head is tilted sideways and often a clicking of the tongue is done. Smiles, however, are universal and, if in doubt, smile and see what happens!

LOOKING AT EUROPE

Most people will be in agreement with the statement that latin types (Spaniards, Italians, etc.) tend to be rather flamboyant and lively.

Not only are hand gestures more noticeable, but the zoning areas are different. Italians tend to stand really close to people when in conversation, while to the British that would be invading a personal zoning area. Similarly there will be more touching, probably because they are close enough to be able to do this more effectively, and their general posture will be relaxed, although by nature these can be quite hot-headed people. Should an Italian or Spaniard be seen putting their forefinger under their eye and pulling down at the skin to make the eye wider, this signals that they feel it is necessary to keep awake and alert, whilst in countries such as France and Germany, the meaning would be that the person was already alert and missing nothing. Italians who wish to convey the message to be alert will tap their nose, whilst to those of us in Britain, this could mean that we are indicating that a subject is confidential, although if this nose tap were used as a result of the question 'What's happening?' the meaning could be taken as 'mind your own business and keep your nose out'.

Greek people are also quite expressive in their facial gestures, and the amount of eye contact they have with both friends and strangers is quite considerable, so that those who don't have a lot of eye contact with them may even be considered ignorant.

Looking towards Germany, stance is generally more erect, and zoning areas will be enlarged so that people do not appear to be standing too closely together. German people are not necessarily very tactile. The Nordic countries do not tend to make a lot of eye contact and, in fact, studies have shown that in Sweden, people look at each other less than in any other European country. Maybe this is why people in Sweden tend to be less inhibited, leading to nudism becoming accepted, even on television programmes.

Looking at Asia and Arabia

Japanese people are by nature very formal in approach, and eye contact and touching will be minimal. Family structures are quite rigid, and the father, as head of the household, will always walk in

front of the women and children. Conformity, and hence, uniforms are commonplace. The Japanese bow when introduced to people, smiles and laughter are rare in public places, although they are far more relaxed and happy looking in business situations. Many Japanese people will sit crossed legged on the floor to eat, and table heights are very low indeed.

To the Japanese, the art of scratching the head means anger, whilst to most Western people, this merely shows confusion. As a result, this movement is something to be avoided in business situations, as the signals can be misread by the Japanese.

Arab people like to maintain eye contact as much as possible, and an Arab will be quite put out if he is unable to see the eyes of the person he wishes to talk to. As a result Arab people stand very close to other people when in conversation, sometimes too close for comfort where more distant zoning areas are the norm. An Arab will be quite ill at ease in conversation with someone who is wearing sunglasses, as he will just not be able to see the eyes. As with the latin races, Arab people are quite tactile and generally expressive emotionally, although it is not permissable for an Arab woman to be touched in public and they must be covered from head to foot with only their eyes visible.

Using the television and video to help you

Before we end our initial journey of discovery, start thinking about all you have learnt. Start to observe and practise various elements of body language, and note the results.

People-watching can be a very entertaining and interesting practice. Confidence, especially, is something which is easy to spot, and those of us who feel shy or inferior in any way at all would do well to study the behaviour and body language of those who ooze confidence, and see how they act and interact with others.

One really good way of studying body language without being observed is by watching television chat shows. If you have access to a video recorder, I would strongly suggest that you video the event. Many chat shows, especially American ones, will have themes – and often these programmes will bring the whole range of personal emotions and situations right into our living room, as well as also bringing us into contact with other people from different cultures and backgrounds. When you watch a programme as it happens, you may not necessarily be in a position to monitor as closely as you would wish the different types of body language being displayed. However, if you can video the programme and watch it through afterwards, with the added benefit of having seen the programme already and knowing the people and their problems, you will be able to spot all sorts of different body-language aspects, and make appropriate notes.

You may also wish to start filming your family, especially when they are unaware of your filming, and see for yourself all their little traits and ways of behaving. Even with people we know well, we often find ourselves noticing things we had failed to notice before, and learn from that. Similarly, you may wish to start turning down the sound on films, especially if you have seen the film before, and look at how actors portray certain characters. See for yourself whether that character behaviour is correct. Often when we are watching films, we merely listen to the dialogue, or concentrate in the main on this, and fail to spot the movements and gestures made. Watch for differences in race, sex and types of people. However, if using cinema films, plays and the like, do remember that these people are acting, and some are better at it than others.

Remember throughout your subsequent studies that even experts in body language don't know everything – we are all on a learning curve, and there is always new information to assimilate and learn. Just keep on observing and have fun with it!

fURTHER READING
AND RESOURCES

Argyle, Michael, *The Psychology of Interpersonal Behaviour*, Penguin, 1972

Hall, E. T., *Silent Language*, Doubleday and Co., New York, 1959

Jourard, Sidney, *Self-disclosure*, Wiley, 1971

Jourard, Sidney, *The Transparent Self*, Van Nostrand, New York, 1964

Lamb, Warren, *Posture and Gesture*, Duckworth, 1965

Morris, Desmond, *Gestures*, Cape, 1979

Morris, Desmond, *Manwatching*, Cape, 1977

Morris, Desmond, *The Human Zoo*, McGraw-Hill, New York, 1969

Morris, Desmond, *The Naked Ape*, McGraw-Hill, New York, 1967

Warfel, Harry R., *A Science of Human Behaviour*, Howard Allen, Cleveland, 1962

Other titles in this series

Astral Projection Is it possible for the soul to leave the body at will? In this book the traditional techniques used to achieve astral projection are described in a simple, practical way, and Out of the Body and Near Death Experiences are also explored.

Astrology An exploration of how astrology helps us to understand ourselves and other people. Learn how to draw up and interpret a horoscope.

Astrology and Health This book explains simply the symbolic richness of the zodiac signs and how they can illuminate our experience of health.

Becoming Prosperous A guide to how *anyone* can feel and become more prosperous by focusing on state of mind and conscious thought. Practical exercises help readers develop personal strategies to become more prosperous, both financially and emotionally.

Chakras The body's energy centres, the chakras, can act as gateways to healing and increased self-knowledge. This book shows you how to work with chakras in safety and with confidence.

Channelling Channelling is the process by which ancient knowledge and wisdom are tapped and reclaimed for the enlightenment and enrichment of life in the present. This book offers simple techniques to become channels of awareness.

Chinese Horoscopes In the Chinese system of horoscopes, the year of birth is all-important. *Chinese Horoscopes for beginners* tells you how to determine your own Chinese horoscope, what personality traits you are likely to have, and how your fortunes may fluctuate in years to come.

Dowsing People all over the world have used dowsing since the earliest times. This book shows how to start dowsing – what to use, what to dowse, and what to expect when subtle energies are detected.

Dream Interpretation This fascinating introduction to the art and science of dream interpretation explains how to unravel the meaning behind dream images to interpret your own and other people's dreams.

Earth Mysteries What can we learn from observing the earth and the remains of our prehistoric ancestors? Explore ley lines, earth energies, astro-archaeology and sacred landscapes to expand your consciousness and achieve a better perspective on existence.

Enlightenment Learn how you can experience primary enlightenment through tried-and-tested exercises which offer the tools to help you to find your own unique truth.

Feng Shui This beginner's guide to the ancient art of luck management will show you how to increase your good fortune and well-being by harmonising your environment with the natural energies of the earth.

Freeing Your Intuition Develop awareness of your intuition and make your own good fortune, increase your creative output and learn to recognise what you *know*, not just what you think.

Gems and Crystals For centuries gems and crystals have been used as an aid to healing and meditation. This guide tells you all you need to know about choosing, keeping and using stones to increase your personal awareness and improve your well-being.

Ghosts In this exploration of the shadowy world of ghosts, the author looks at poltergeists, hauntings, ghouls, phantoms of the living, the ouija board, ghost hunting, scientific proof of survival after death and the true meaning of Hallowe'en.

The Goddess This book traces the development, demise and rebirth of the Goddess, looking at the worship of Her and retelling myths from all over the world.

Graphology Graphology, the science of interpreting handwriting to reveal personality, is now widely accepted and used throughout the world. This introduction will enable you to make a comprehensive analysis of your own and other people's handwriting to reveal the hidden self.

The Healing Powers of Plants Plants and herbs can be used to enhance everyday life through aromatherapy, herbalism, homoeopathy and colour therapy. Their power can be used in cosmetics, meditation and home decoration.

Herbs for Magic and Ritual This book looks at the well-known herbs and the stories attached to them. There is information on the use of herbs in essential oils and incense, and on their healing and magical qualities.

I Ching The roots of *I Ching* or the *Book of Changes* lie in the time of the feudal mandarin lords of China, but its traditional wisdom is still relevant today. Using the original poetry in its translated form, this introduction traces its history, survival and modern-day applications.

Interpreting Signs and Symbols The history of signs and symbols is traced in this book from their roots to the modern age. It also examines the way psychiatry uses symbolism, and the significance of doodles.

The Language of Flowers Flowers can and do heal us, both emotionally and physically, with their smell and their beauty. By looking at these areas, together with superstitions associated with flowers and their links with New Age subjects, the author gives advice on how to enhance your life with flowers.

Love Signs This is a practical introduction to the astrology of romantic relationships. It explains the different roles played by each of the planets, focusing particularly on the position of the Moon at the time of birth.

The Magic and Mystery of Trees This book explores the many meanings of trees, from myth and folklore through ritual and seasonal uses to their 'spiritual essence' and esoteric meanings.

Meditation This beginner's guide gives simple, clear instructions to enable you to start meditating and benefiting from this ancient mental discipline immediately. The text is illustrated throughout by full-colour photographs and line drawings.

Mediumship Whether you want to become a medium yourself, or simply understand what mediumship is about, this book will give you the grounding to undertake a journey of discovery into the spirit realms.

The Moon and You The phase of the Moon when you were born radically affects your personality. This book looks at nine lunar types – how they live, love, work and play, and provides simple tables to find out the phase of your birth.

Norse Tradition This book gives a comprehensive introduction to the Norse Tradition, a vibrant, living current within the multitude of spiritual paths of Paganism.

Numerology Despite being scientifically based, numerology requires no great mathematical talents to understand. This introduction gives you all the information you will need to understand the significance of numbers in your everyday life.

Numerology and Relationships This guide takes you step by step through the hidden meanings behind the important numbers in your life to discover more about you, your compatibilities with others and the crucial relationships with your parents, partner and children.

Pagan Gods for Today's Man Looking at ancient gods and old stories, this guide explores the social and psychological issues affecting the role of men today. In these pages men of all ages and persuasions can find inspiration.

Paganism Pagans are true Nature worshippers who celebrate the cycles of life. This guide describes pagan festivals and rituals and takes a detailed look at the many forms of paganism practised today.

Palmistry Palmistry is the oldest form of character reading still in use. This illustrated guide shows you exactly what to look for and how to interpret what you find.

Qabalah The Qabalah is an ancient Jewish system of spiritual knowledge centred on the Tree of Life. This guide explains how it can be used in meditation and visualisation, and links it to the chakras, yoga, colour therapy, crystals, Tarot and numerology.

Reiki In this book you will find advice on how to learn Reiki, its application and potential, and you will be shown an avenue of understanding of this simple, practical technique which offers pain relief through meditation and laying-on of hands.

Reincarnation and You What happens to us after death? Here, you will find practical advice on using dreams, recurrent visions, déjà vu and precognition to access hidden parts of your consciousness which recall or anticipate past and future lives.

Runes The power of the runes in healing and giving advice about relationships and life in general has been acknowledged since the time of the Vikings. This book shows how runes can be used in our technological age to increase personal awareness and stimulate individual growth.

Shamanism Shamanic technique offers direct contact with Spirit, vivid self-knowledge and true kinship with plants, animals and the planet Earth. This book describes the shamanic way, the wisdom of the Medicine Wheel and power animals.

Some Traditional African Beliefs Fortune telling and healing are two of the aspects of traditional African spiritual life looked at in this book. Exercises based on ancient beliefs show you how to use the environment to find ways to harmonise modern urban life in a practical way.

Spiritual Healing All healing starts with self, and the Universal Power which makes this possible is available to everyone. In this book there are exercises, techniques and guidelines to follow which will enable you to heal yourself and others spiritually.

Star Signs This detailed analysis looks at each of the star signs in turn and reveals how your star sign affects everything about you. This book shows you how to use this knowledge in your relationships and in everyday life.

Tantric Sexuality Tantric Buddhists use sex as a pleasurable path to enlightenment. This guide offers a radically different and exciting new dimension to sex, explaining practical techniques in a clear and simple way.

Tarot Tarot cards have been used for many centuries. This guide gives advice on which sort to buy, where to get them and how to use them. The emphasis is on using the cards positively, as a tool for gaining self-knowledge, while exploring present and future possibilities.

Visualisation This introduction to visualisation, a form of self-hypnosis widely used by Buddhists, will show you how to practise the basic techniques – to relieve stress, improve your health and increase your sense of personal well-being.

Witchcraft This guide to the ancient religion based on Nature worship answers many of the questions and uncovers the myths and misconceptions surrounding witchcraft. Mystical rituals and magic are explained and there is advice for the beginner on how to celebrate the Sabbats.

Working With Colour Colour is the medicine of the future. This book explores the energy of each colour and its significance, gives advice on how colour can enhance our well-being, and gives ideas on using colour in the home and garden.

Your Psychic Powers Are you psychic? This book will help you find out by encouraging you to look more deeply within yourself. Psychic phenomena such as precognitive dreams, out of body travels and visits from the dead are also discussed in this ideal stepping stone towards a more aware you.

To order this series

All books in this series are available from bookshops or, in case of difficulty, can be ordered direct from the publisher. Prices and availability subject to change without notice. Send your order with your name and address to: Hodder & Stoughton Ltd, Cash Sales Department, Bookpoint, 39 Milton Park, Abingdon, OXON, OX14 4TD, UK. If you have a credit card you may order by telephone – 01235 831700.

For sales in the following countries please contact:
UNITED STATES: Trafalgar Square (Vermont), Tel: 800 423 4525 (toll-free)
CANADA: General Publishing (Ontario), Tel: 445 3333
AUSTRALIA: Hodder & Stoughton (Sydney), Tel: 02 638 5299